'HOW TO'
BOOK
OF
BREADMAKING

MALCOLM HOLLOWAY

BLANDFORD PRESS

The **'HOW TO'** Book of Bread and Breadmaking explains in straightforward terms, through the use of concise texts, charts, photographs and diagrams, the methods and techniques that will make your baking more productive and satisfying.

'HOW TO'

Contents

What is bread?	6
Breadmaking in the past	8
Commercial baking	10
Grains for bread	12
Milling	14
Tools and equipment	16
Flours for bread	18
Other ingredients	24
Choice of loaf	30
Basic techniques	32
Method 1	40
Method 2	42
Method 3	44
Traditional recipes	46
Special recipes	52
Twisted and plaited loaves	62
Fruit breads and tea cakes	69
International recipes	78
Fault finding	88
Glossary	92
Index	94

The 'How To' Book of Bread and
Breadmaking was conceived, edited and designed by
Simon Jennings and Company Limited,
42 Maiden Lane, London WC2, England.

Conceived & Designed by Simon Jennings
General Editor: Michael Bowers
Designer & Researcher: Caroline Courtney
Text: Malcolm Holloway
Illustrations: Lindsay Blow
Special Photography: John Couzins

First published in the United Kingdom 1981 by Blandford Press
Copyright © 1981 Blandford Books Ltd.

American edition:
distributed in the United States by
Sterling Publishing Co., Inc.
Two Park Avenue, New York N.Y. 10016

Distributed in Canada by:
Oak Tree Press Limited
c/o Canadian Manda Group
215 Lakeshore Boulevard East
Toronto, Ontario, Canada.

Text and Illustrations Copyright
© 1981 Simon Jennings and Company Limited

0-8069-9690-0

*All rights reserved. No part of
this book may be reproduced
or transmitted in any form or by
any means, electronic or
mechanical, including
photocopying, recording or any
information storage and
retrieval system, without
permission in writing from the
publisher.*

Printed in Singapore

THE AUTHOR

Malcolm Holloway is exceptionally well qualified to write on the subject of breadmaking, being a Master Baker and the proprietor of two bakeries in Yorkshire, England. His professional interests are wide ranging: as well as coping with the demands of an expanding business, which involves many aspects of the catering trade, he also finds time to be a frequent radio broadcaster on matters relating to food and wine.

Introduction

The purpose of this book is to help both the novice and experienced baker to understand more fully the effects that raw materials, temperatures, processes and moisture levels have upon the bread you bake. The emphasis of this book, as the title suggests, is on the 'how to' of baking bread. There are many recipe books for the aspiring baker, and it is true that there is a section of this book devoted to recipes. However, the recipes in this small volume are intended to be basic ideas which can be varied by the baker. With nearly all the recipes there are several variations of bread which can be produced from them. The baker may wish to use other favorite or interesting recipes to make the various breads described in this book and I applaud the initiative of the baker who does.

Do try to read the first half of this book, which is devoted to the understanding of baking, first. If you decide to learn to bake then, you will discover that much of the myth of bread production will disappear, and what at first appeared to be complex and mysterious really comes down to obvious common sense. Once you have reached that stage you will be able to invent and adapt your own recipes and you will impress your family and friends with your skill and competence.

This book will not make you into a good baker, only you can do that, but I hope it will be a good base from which to begin or further your understanding and skill in a very absorbing and much appreciated craft.

An old baker once described the baker's job as *'making water stand up'*. On a commercial level this is probably true, but I feel that bread baking gives fulfilment and satisfaction to the baker and a lot of enjoyment and gastronomic pleasure to the recipients.

Happy Baking!

What is bread?

Bread is, quite simply, the baked product of ground, milled grain. Throughout the world this can take many forms, but in the West we tend to regard the fermentation process as an integral part of breadmaking, other forms of baking being thought of as flour, confectionary or cake making.

Bread is an important part of our diet and provides many of the essential ingredients for our well-being and good health. Apart from protein, fat, carbohydrates and necessary dietary fibres, bread contains no less than twelve trace elements which we need for the maintenance and fitness of our bodies.

No medically approved diet for weight loss will omit bread completely, for it is not only an excellent source of many of the ingredients which our bodies use so voraciously, but it also contains an anti-depressant which, especially in these days of high intensity living, is so necessary to help prevent us all from finishing up as nervous wrecks.

Nutritionally, bread is as valuable and important today, as it ever was; there is every reason for baking still to be an essential domestic skill.

The many stages of bread
Bread is the end result of a long journey from the wheat lands, typified by these pictures of central France, *right*, and the cigarette card version of the Canadian prairies, *bottom left*. From harvesting, *center left*, to the finished product, *below*, many processes are involved – not least of which is the drying of the grain, usually in ultra-modern granaries like the one at Trondheim, Norway, *top left*.

Breadmaking in the past

Bread, and the craft of making it, are nearly as old as civilized man himself. The earliest evidence of breadmaking was found in caves in Southern France when man first spread to Europe from Africa. Early man cultivated grain, and when it was ripe crushed it between two stones, mixed the 'flour' with water and left the dough on stones to bake in the sun.

In Neolithic times, the baking process was speeded up, by first heating the stones on which the dough was baked and then covering it with hot ashes – a method not recommended to today's aspiring baker.

The Egyptians discovered that if the dough was left to ferment for some time, the resultant bread was lighter and of greater volume, making a much more palatable loaf than before. Ovens were also invented by Egyptians – thus paving the way for a baking industry to develop.

It was the Romans who first turned breadmaking into an important craft. Their tastes were much more sophisticated and demanding than earlier civilizations and Roman millers developed whiter, blander flours, enabling the baker to produce bread which suited the Roman palate. They made not only a very basic loaf, but also a variety of 'fancy' breads containing such things as honey, milk and oil to improve both the flavor and texture in their bread. In the Museum of Naples, examples of bread baked in Pompeii over 2000 years ago, and preserved by the ash of Vesuvius can be seen today, often with the maker's name stamped on it.

Not until the middle of the 17th century was there any further significant improvement in breadmaking. In the 1630's, yeast was used in breadmaking to help develop the fermenting doughs, but until that time 'sour' or old doughs which had been fermenting, in some cases for many years, were added to the bread dough to aid fermentation. This meant that the dough had to rise overnight which made baking a very lengthy process. This method of baking is still used in some places, mainly Scotland, and produces a very nice loaf.

Until relatively recent times, all bread produced in Europe was of the wholewheat type which is enjoying a revival today. This type of bread has little volume compared to the standard loaf available today, because it is made from soft European wheats which have a low gluten content – the dough, therefore, has little elasticity and will collapse before it achieves much in the way of volume. Wheats which have a high gluten, or protein, content allow the yeast to develop the dough to a much greater extent and produce the type of loaf which is in general use today.

Primeval baking
We will never know precisely how bread was made in the Stone Age, but we can be fairly certain that it was not remotely like this romanticized vision. Possibly the artist did not have sufficient knowledge of breadmaking in his own time to be able to make a reasonable guess at its origins.

Commercial baking

Over 70% of bread produced today comes from the large commercial bakeries, belonging to the international combines. The loaves they produce can be found on any supermarket shelf, in all their pre-packaged glory. However, the small or medium sized bakery would seem to be enjoying a resurgence.

All bakeries today rely on highly sophisticated machinery which, contrary to general belief, requires an even higher standard of skill, technical as well as craft, from the Master Baker than ever before.

There are now many small bakeries everywhere which cater admirably to the more discerning customer. The standard of bread and other baked goods obtainable from these small bakeries is very high, and the range of breads now on general sale is the widest ever offered to the customer.

Many years of skill and experience are the heritage of today's Master Baker. This, combined with the modern technical advances now available, enables the baker of the 80's to provide a far better and more complete service to his customer than his predecessor ever could.

Bakers of the world
Commercial baking has a long history and, although there may appear to be little in common between the French bakery of the turn of the century, *above right*, and the vast modern ovens, *below right*, the principles of baking remain the same. Geography, too, makes little difference. The scene in a middle-eastern rising room, *below*, can be observed in small bakeries all over the world. On the grand scale, *top left*, commercial baking can seem rather sterile. Most people prefer the atmosphere of the small shop, *center and bottom left*.

Grains for bread

Throughout the world, several different grains or cereals are used in the manufacture of many different types of localized bread. Corn (maize), barley, millet and buckwheat are all used, although the end product would not be recognized as bread to those of us used to the more commonly known product of wheat and rye. In India, the locally grown millet is the most important grain and is used to produce millet cakes and chapatis. Tortillas (made from maize) are common to Latin America. These and other similar flat loaves found throughout the world are gaining in popularity in the modern Western convenience-orientated society.

However, the cereals inherent to Europe and North America are rye and wheat, the latter being by far the most popular medium for breadmaking and baking generally.

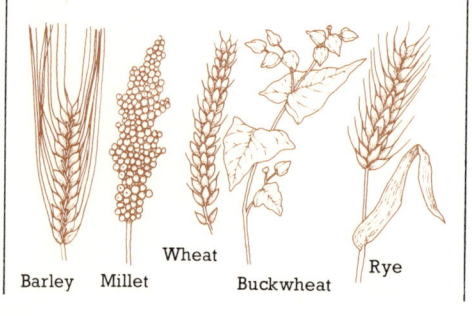

The suitability of wheat lies in its protein content, which is known as *gluten*, and here rests the crux of the matter. Gluten is an elastic-like substance which has the quality of being able to stretch and hold, rather like a good girdle. This elasticity is an essential quality in breadmaking when it was learned that allowing the dough to ferment produced gasses (even more so during the advent of yeast) it became necessary to hold them in the dough – thus allowing it to rise. Gluten has this ability to hold the gasses produced and so make the whole process of breadmaking into the art and industry it is today. It can be observed, through experiment, that the more gluten is developed the more its elastic qualities are engendered – thus the necessity for kneading dough.

Rye grain has a much lower gluten content than wheat grain, yet it has its own properties of flavor and food content which many people prefer. When it is used with wheat flour in varying proportions it can be made into a large variety of bread products.

Barley   Millet   Wheat   Buckwheat   Rye

Starch or Endosperm
The soft chalky white substance that most of us would immediately recognize as flour, and is the part most prized by millers for use in modern bakeries for white bread manufacture.

Germ
Germ is only a small percentage of the whole grain, but is where all the richest food value is found. However, much of the germ is lost in white flour production through the milling process.

Bran (Pericarp)
The protective hard skin around the seed has for many years been regarded as useless for nutritional purposes and a nuisance in bread production. Bran has, therefore, been discarded by miller and baker alike. For years it was only used in the manufacture of animal feed stuff – apart from a small amount retained for sale through health food shops. However, more recent medical opinion has proved that eating bran in a normal diet is positively advantageous to health, combating constipation and ailments such as obesity and heart disease which may directly or indirectly derive from it.

WHAT IS GRAIN?

Grain, quite simply, is the seed of a cereal plant; cereals are those plants which are loosely described as corn. Wheat, maize, barley, millet, buckwheat and rye are the chief cereals and the seeds, or grains, of all can be ground to produce a flour. Only the flour produced by wheat and rye, however, is really suitable for breadmaking.

The beard
This, and any remaining stalk, will usually be discarded during milling.

Bran
Bran is the pericarp, or protective skin of the grain. Nutritionally useless, but valuable as fibre.

Endosperm
This is the inner starchy substance which is the seedling's food supply and the chief ingredient of flour.

The germ
The germ contains the plumule and radicle – the embryo stem and root of the new plant. This is the most nutritious part of the grain.

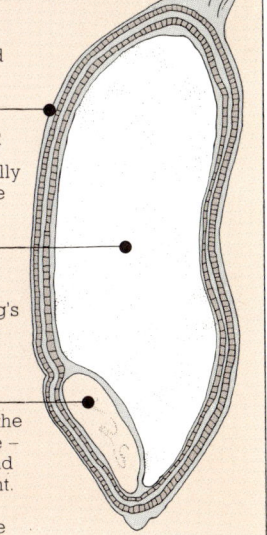

Milling

In one or two isolated places the old fashioned mill can be found, still milling the wheat by the age-old method of grinding it between two huge stones. The stones are placed on top of each other so that the two carefully grooved surfaces meet. The top stone has a hole through the center into which the coarse grain is poured. The stones revolve in opposite directions and the flour is ejected along the grooves and out through the gaps between the stones. The first milling makes a very coarse flour which can only be used in the manufacture of wholewheat bread and is not normally suitable for baking. Therefore, the rough flour is put through the stones again and again, each time becoming finer but losing a little of the wheat germ which sticks to the stones during milling.

The most widely used modern method of milling is roller milling. In this method cleansed grain is passed through chilled iron rollers which crack the wheat and extract the flour from the bran. Further flour is removed by a multi-sifting process, the finest of which is more like silk than a sieve. What is left is the fine white powder which we know as flour.

Mills and millers
In all societies, milling is a traditional skill. From the primitive pounding of the grain in India, *bottom left*, and the equally rustic water mill, *top left*, to the more familiar windmills, *this page*, the principle of grinding the grain to a fine powder remains the same. In India, water is a more reliable means of power than wind, even if the water has to be ducted in a rather unusual way – as in the mill at Aurangabad, *below right*.

Tools & equipment

The equipment normally required for breadmaking can be found in most domestic kitchens. None of the equipment shown here need be bought exclusively for bread and no particular expense need be incurred to become a baker. Even bread tins are not essential; in their place an ordinary cake tin can be used to produce a round loaf, or a deep oblong foil dish may be utilized as a small loaf 'tin'. I have seen sawn-off broom handles used successfully as rolling pins – even in a professional bakery. An old towel folded several times can substitute very well for oven cloths. So do not feel that to become a good baker you need a whole new lot of equipment; the bare essentials and a little initiative will suffice.

The most important points to remember when choosing any new equipment are ease of cleaning and durability. All bakery equipment must be kept clean and this includes hands, for dough will find and pick up any pieces of foreign matter on equipment and incorporate it in the bread.

If you are considering investing in new bread tins buy a good quality tin which will last a long time. The tin you use will have to withstand prolonged heat, so do not purchase one which will leave flakes of alloy paint on the sides of your loaf.

If you are using new tins for your loaf, they will have to be 'baked out' before you use them for bread. Baking out means that the new tin should spend several hours in a hot oven.

It is not necessary to waste a lot of gas or electricity exclusively for this use, but in the course of your normal cooking or baking pop the tins into any spare part of the oven and leave them. If you can spare the space leave them there for a week. Never wash bread tins but wipe them out well with a dry cloth kept for the purpose.

TOOLS AND EQUIPMENT

The basic bread-making kit is very simple and will suffice for all of the recipes given in this book.

Mixing bowls
Mixing bowls should be big enough to hold several cups of flour and allow sufficient space for hand mixing.

Rolling pin
The standard wooden rolling pin shown here is suitable for almost any baking job.

Measuring cup
Essential for all liquid ingredients.

Sieve
Sifting of the dry ingredients is always a good idea in baking.

Spoons
Useful for measuring small quantities of ingredients.

Scales
Weighing ingredients is an unavoidable part of breadmaking.

Flours for bread

The choice of flour now available to the breadmaker is probably wider and more easily obtainable than ever before. Millers seem to have realized that people are more discerning about the bread they eat and demand a much wider choice of flavors and textures from the flours they buy.

White flours

The flour most easily obtainable at your local supermarket is likely to be the produce of one of the large combines who tend to produce a general baking flour which, although it is an excellent medium for pastries, cakes etc., does not have the high gluten content which is more desirable for breadmaking, but when used in quick breads can produce excellent results.

Many mills produce a bread flour for the domestic market. These flours are easily distinguished from the weaker flours by the emphasis the labelling gives to the inclusion of Canadian or North American wheats. These flours are very good for breadmaking because of their relatively high protein content and will allow the bread made with them to have higher volume, better texture, whiter color and longer keeping qualities.

Cereal growing
A great deal of research is conducted into the growing of cereals on experimental farms like the one shown above. These, and the modern methods of milling shown in the other picture, ensure that the flour which goes into our bread is of the highest quality. The opposite page shows a number of the principal grains and the flours milled from them.

19

Brown flours

Brown flours are available in a wide range of types; the one you choose is really a matter of personal taste. Some ordinary brown flours are colored white flours but these are, thank goodness, disappearing from the shops because most people who want to make brown bread want something a little better than the tasteless sliced variety sold for many years by the large bakers.

Germ meal or *wheat meal* flours have also been a popular choice for a long time. These are brown flours which have extra wheat germ added by the millers. Many manufacturers of germ meals also add salt during production – so check the wrapper. Loaves made from germ meal flours have a moister texture and much more flavor than the ordinary brown flours. Most people will have tried bread produced from germ meals, for the loaves made from this flour have the same name as the flour irrespective of who manufactures the bread. Widespread advertising ensures that flour of this type is a household name, for example: *'Don't say brown, say . . .'*

Constituents of flours used in breadmaking

This table shows the main components of commonly used flours. Essential ingredients not shown are Calcium, Iron, Thiamin, Nicotinic Acid and Riboflavin. Flours below the 80% extraction level have these nutrients added after milling to restore the level.

	Usual extraction rate percent	Protein percent	Fat percent	Carbohydrate percent	Crude fibre percent	Dietary fibre	Additives
WHITE	72	11.3	1.0	71.5	0.12	3.15	Chalk and nutrients
BROWN	85–90	12.0	2.4	64.3	2.0	11.2	Chalk
WHOLEWHEAT	100	12.0	2.4	64.3	2.0	11.2	Nil
WHOLEWHEAT *All-British wheat*	100	8.9	2.2	67.0	1.8	11.2	Nil

Based on figures supplied by the British Flour Advisory Bureau

Wholewheat flours

Wholewheat flours are growing faster in popularity than any other, following the trend to a more natural diet for healthier living. Wholewheats are just that, the whole wheat grain excluding the bran or husk which is the hard skin of the wheat. Most of the wholewheats available are milled in the normal process with the extract, which is lost in normal roller milling, given back to the finished flour. Wholewheat loaves have a much stronger flavor than ordinary brown bread although they have much less volume and feel heavy in comparison.

Another variation on wholewheat is *stone ground* flour which is milled in the traditional way between two large mill stones and has quite a distinct flavor. The texture is much coarser than flours produced by the more widely used roller method of milling.

Granary flour is wholewheat flour, often part stone ground with the bran added, giving a nice nutty flavor to the loaf.

Wholewheat flours are gradually creeping into use and although distribution is not widespread, its popularity is increasing. If you can get *wholewheat* you will discover a new experience in bread. The flour is simply the whole of the wheat, often organically grown, stone ground with nothing added or extracted. Bread produced from this flour is very low in volume, about half the size of a normal loaf, and completely different in flavor. It is very easy to make and delightful to eat.

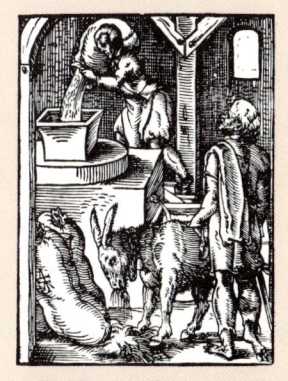

Der Müller.

Wer Korn vnd Weitz zu malen hat/
Der bring mirs in die Mül herab/
Denn schütt ichs zwischen den Mülstein
Vnd mal es sauber rein vnd klein/
Die Kleyen gib ich treuwlich zu/
Hirsch/Erbeiß/ich auch neuwen thu/
Dergleich thu ich auch Stockfisch bleuwn/
Würtz stoß ich auch mit gantzn treuwen.
                                    Der

Loaf textures

The texture of a loaf is largely conditioned by the flour used in the baking, although the use of fats, milk, eggs and other enriching ingredients, can have a considerable effect. The open, light texture associated with white bread is due to the extra volume achieved by the high gluten content. *Brown*, or *wheatmeal*, flours result in a closer texture and slightly heavier bread. Wholewheat which has been roller milled is much more dense and has about half the volume of a white loaf. *Stone ground wholewheat* is coarser than the commercial wholewheat but similar in density or volume.

Texture contrast ▶
The breads shown on the right can all be made using the recipes in this book. This picture clearly shows the open texture of the white flours contrasted with the lower volume and denser texture of the brown, wholewheat and rye flours.

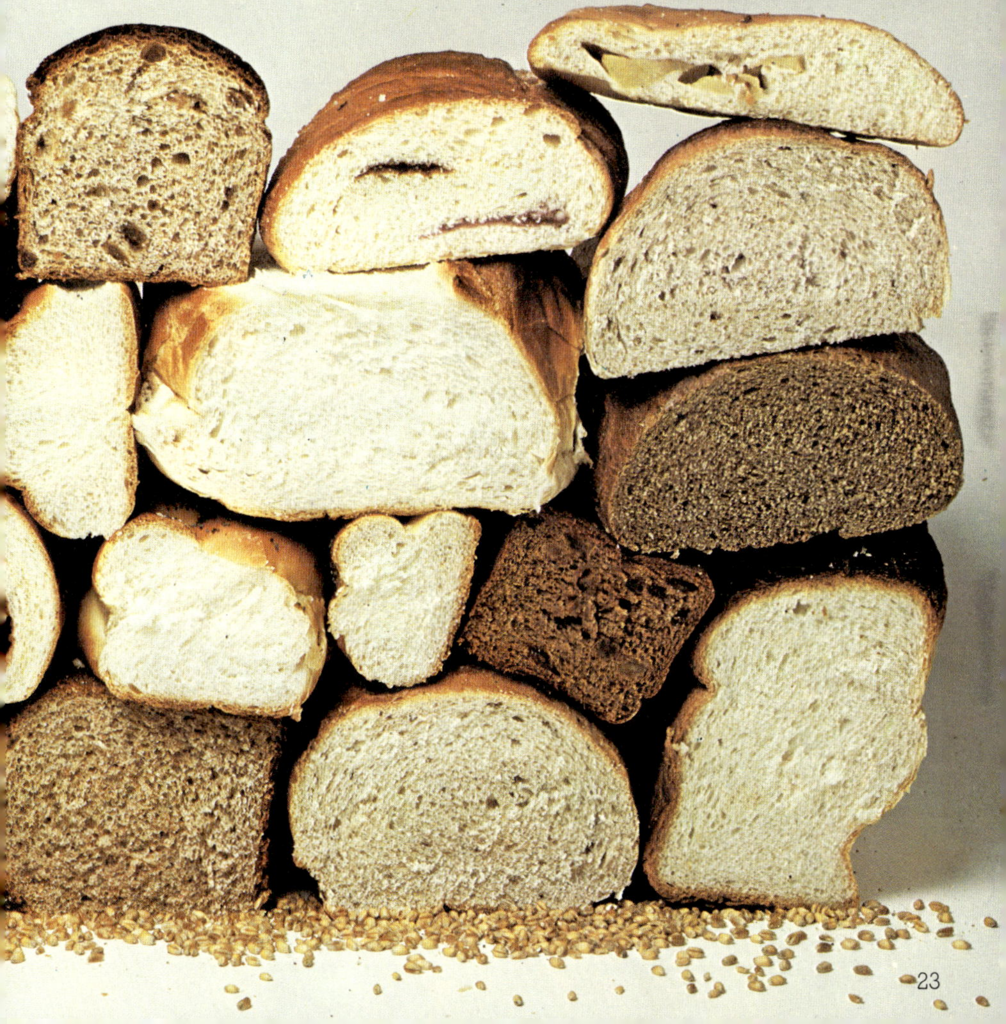

The other ingredients

The basic ingredients used in bread making are flour, water, yeast and salt. With these four ingredients an amazing variety of breads can be made. However, color, texture and flavor can be improved or altered with the addition of sugar, fats, milk, malt and eggs. Below is a list of ingredients together with the effects they will produce and the quantities that should be used.

Ascorbic Acid (Vitamin C)

This is well known to bakers and is used all the time in large plant bakeries, and often in smaller bakeries, where the high speed method of production is used.

The quality which is inherent in vitamin C is that of helping the gluten in the flour to develop quickly, ensuring that the dough made with added vitamin C requires no bulk fermentation time and has, therefore, much less tendency to scum – especially if it is made up in a drafty or cool room.

Vitamin C is an essential element in your diet, helping to combat the common cold and to promote general good health. There is widening medical opinion that a good vitamin C intake also helps to ward off cancer in its various forms. So apart from assisting your breadmaking the use of vitamin C is an excellent way of incorporating this highly beneficial vitamin into your family's diet.

Probably the best way to add vitamin C, or ascorbic acid, to your dough is in the form of effervescent vitamin C tablets which are available at your pharmacy. To every two cups of water add two tablets before the sugar and yeast. Then put the mixture directly into the flour and mix in the normal fashion. When mixed, there is no need to leave your dough in bulk fermentation, just cut and mould it then let rise and bake as normal.

To adapt any of the methods in this book to include vitamin C, follow the method given and simply cut out the bulk fermentation, or leavening, which is shown to be required in the recipe.

Table Salt

Essential for flavor because bread without salt is quite tasteless. It also controls the volume of the loaf and adds to the color. Salt should be used at a rate of 26g (1½ Tbs) per 1.35kg of flour. Too much salt will reduce the volume of the loaf and retard fermentation, resulting in a very highly colored loaf with a salty flavor.

Fats
Fats improve flavor, keeping qualities and texture. Any type of fat – oil, butter, margarine, white fat or lard may be used. However, in the case of butter and margarine remember that the normal variety contains salt, and therefore, the salt content of the bread should be reduced slightly. In most recipes 30g (2 Tbs) of fat to 1.35kg (12 cups) flour is the usage rate, though in some specialty breads the rate is greatly increased – in these the yeast content is increased because fat acts as a retardant in the fermentation process.

Granulated Sugar
Sugar will speed up fermentation and improve flavor, color and keeping qualities. It will also produce a softer crust. Quantities again vary depending on the type of loaf required, but 30g (2 Tbs) per 1.35kg (12 cups) is about the normal usage rate. Sugar should never in any circumstances be mixed directly with yeast because raw sugar kills yeast, but it should be added to the liquid for the odd-sounding reason that sugar mixed with liquid changes from a yeast killer to a yeast food. Recipes requiring high sugar will need less liquid and more yeast.

Milk
Can replace water completely, or in varying proportions, and can be added in powder form. Milk will improve flavor and give a high color to the crust which will also be softened.

Malt
Used mainly in brown breads to improve flavor and baking qualities. Usually, malt is added in the milling process but a little liquid malt can be added to the water content to increase nutritional value.

Eggs
Eggs will improve flavor, texture and nutritional value. They should be used sparingly: to 1.35kg (12 cups) of flour replace 6cl (¼ cup) of the liquid with one egg for a very much enriched loaf.

Yeast
Yeast is the essence of breadmaking; see page 28 for a detailed explanation of its importance.

Festive & special loaves

Bread, especially leavened bread, has been associated with festive occasions since very early times. Perhaps the most important event calling for special breads is Easter. There may be some deliberate association between the action of yeast in dough and the religious significance of the festival. Certainly, Easter breads are traditional in many parts of the world – particularly in Greece, Italy and Russia, while England has its hot cross buns, Poland an Easter ring and Germany a special fruit loaf.

Harvest time is another occasion for festive breadmaking. In Britain and America this often takes the form of elaborate designs in dough – depicting wheatsheafs, animals and country scenes. Such loaves are more for decoration, and to demonstrate the skill of the baker and the versatility of bread dough, than for eating.

Christmas and the New Year bring on a great spate of cakes, buns and breads. Holland, Germany and Austria are the homes of scores of yeast cakes, fruit loaves and (especially Austria) the delicious stollen. Many of the specialties included in this book have festive origins and are still associated with annual celebrations.

Special breads
Bread is such a basic commodity that it figures in countless cultural and religious festivals. The ceremony of blessing the hot cross buns in London, *above*, and the tribal celebration *right*, are both concerned with thanksgiving. Even the maize granary on the Canary Islands, *above right*, has religious connections. Festival breads on sale in Munich, *top left*, and Marrakesh, *bottom left*, may taste different but they serve the same purpose.

Yeast & breadmaking

Yeast

Without yeast as an aid to fermentation, bread as we know it would not exist. Yeast should be treated carefully and never be introduced to salt, raw sugar or water temperatures above 49°C (120°F) because all these will kill the yeast cell. Yeast in good condition should feel cold and firm to the touch and should have a pleasant fresh odor. If it is kept in the refrigerator at about 3° to 4°C (38° to 40°F) it will stay in good condition for two to three weeks. Once the yeast has begun to deteriorate, the outer edges will discolor, and it will crumble easily and smell rather unpleasant. In this condition it will be of little use in breadmaking.

Yeast quantities vary enormously according to fermentation times, room, flour and water temperatures, sugar, salt and fat contents and the qualities of the yeast used. On average, yeast will be used at the rate of 15–30g (1–2 Tbs) per 450g (4 cups) of flour but, as previously stated, will vary enormously according to the recipe. Dried yeast is more concentrated than fresh yeast and should be used at half the rate indicated in the recipes. Use it only if you cannot get fresh yeast.

WHAT IS YEAST?

This question can be simply answered by saying that yeast is a plant. It is, however, a very special kind of plant – one that can turn starches and sugars into alcohol. This is the process which is known as fermentation. Fermentation is the most vital process in the business of breadmaking. In breadmaking, alcohol is less important than the carbondioxide which is produced during fermentation – it is this which gives the bread its volume.

OTHER INGREDIENTS

There is practically no limit to the ingredients which may be used in breadmaking, but those shown here are commonly used and can be incorporated with the dough.

Dried fruit
Currants, white and dark raisins are familiar in many kinds of bread, but dates apricots and prunes can also be used.

Spices
Many spices have been used in bread over the centuries. Cinnamon, caraway seeds, nutmeg and saffron are among the most common.

Malt
The flavor of malt is not to everyone's taste but its addition as malted meal or extracts can make an interesting loaf.

Cream
Although cream is seldom specified in recipes, it can be used in place of other fats to enrich the loaf.

Choice of loaf

In addition to the basic skills and techniques, described in the step-by-step sequences, this book contains over 30 recipes for different kinds of bread and yeast cakes. All of them are shown on this page. These form a basis from which many variations can be made.

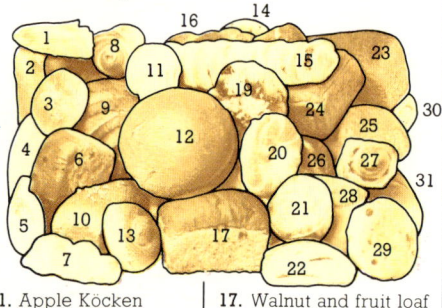

1. Apple Köcken
2. Beer bread
3. Bagels
4. Oven bottom cakes
5. Crumpets
6. Bara-brith
7. Corkscrews and twists
8. French bread
9. Bloomer
10. Wholewheat
11. Brioche
12. Round loaf
13. Coils
14. Chelsea tea ring
15. Lattice tea bread
16. Three strand plait
17. Walnut and fruit loaf
18. Hot cross buns
19. Fruit plaits
20. Croissants
21. Muffins
22. Cinnamon slice
23. Brown loaf
24. Fruit malt bread
25. Rye bread
26. Fourpiece
27. Sticky buns
28. Cottage
29. Yorkshire tea cake
30. Stollen
31. Sweet and sour

31

TECHNIQUES

Step-by-step breadmaking	32
Rising	36
Kneading and moulding	38
Straight dough – method I	40
Ferment and dough – method 2	42
Flying sponge – method 3	44

Basic techniques

The following pages show in detail the skills and methods needed for basic breadmaking. Step-by-step sequences deal with the procedures that are common to all breadmaking, including the vital elements of rising and kneading.

The section concludes with three methods of mixing the dough – each of them related to recipes which are given later in the book. Oven temperatures, 'Punching down' and the intricacies of moulding dough are all dealt with in a way which makes the subsequent recipes very easy to follow.

Breadmaking – basic procedure

In all methods of breadmaking a certain procedure should be established to help eliminate the more obvious mistakes which can be so easily made by the baker, e.g., omitting the salt or putting it in twice, either way ruining all the hard work put into a loaf. The novice baker will find that writing out the recipe and a timetable for the method, including temperatures, will be a great help.

The method you wish to use, i.e., the straight dough (Method I) or Ferment and Dough (Method II) will determine the sequence of steps to be followed. If Method I is used, then follow the guidance through in sequence. If, however, Method II is employed then stages 5 and 6 should precede steps 3 and 4.

Method:

1. *Assemble all your equipment, making sure that it is thoroughly cleaned and set it out in the order it is required.*

2. *Gather all your ingredients and measure them out in the correct quantities, again arranging them in the correct order.*

3. *Sift the dry ingredients together, i.e., flour, salt, and milk powder (if used).*

4. *Rub the fat into the flour and gather onto the baking surface, making a well in the center. When using a mixer place them in the bowl.*

5. *Add the sugar and yeast to the water. NB: At no time should raw sugar be mixed with the yeast.*

6. *Add the liquid to the dry ingredients and mix. At this point, any extra flour or water can be added depending on the stiffness or slackness of the dough.*

continued on next page

breadmaking
continued

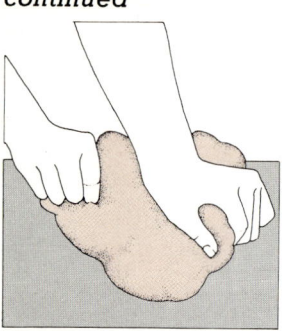

7. Knead the dough with a folding and tearing motion. Don't be afraid of harming the dough – pretend you hate it and give way to an outburst of violence!

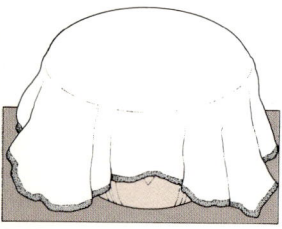

8. Allow the dough to recover by covering and leaving in a warm (not hot), draft-free place for the required time.

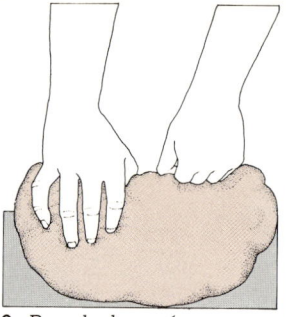

9. Punch down (re-knead) the dough, if required, and cover again until bulk fermentation time is up.

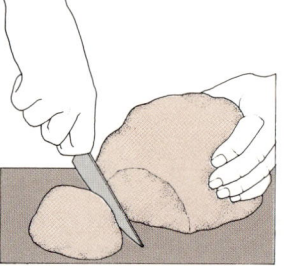

10. Punch down again and cut the dough to the required sizes. It is best to weigh each piece to allow for uniform rising and baking. This is a good time to turn on your oven.

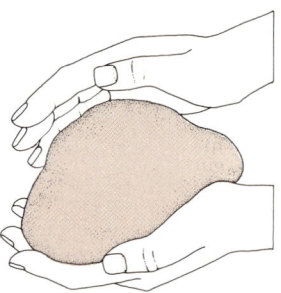

11. Shape the dough by proper moulding – not by gently patting the dough to shape.

12. Place the dough into greased tins or baking sheets or, in the case of dough cakes, roll out with the rolling pin.

13. Set the dough pieces aside in a warm damp, atmosphere – a steamy kitchen or bathroom is ideal. (see Rising page 36).

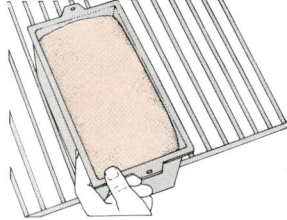

14. Taking great care not to stick your fingers into the now risen dough, nor to knock the tins (if you do the dough will go down like a pricked balloon and will need re-rising, place the dough into the pre-heated oven and bake for the required time, or until the bread is of an even golden color.

15. Remove the bread from the oven and take it out of the tins immediately. Place on to a wire rack allowing plenty of air space all round the loaf until cool.

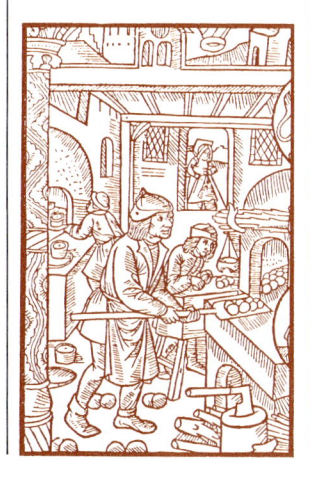

BAKING TIMES

The length of baking time given in the recipes in this book assume that the oven will function efficiently at the temperature indicated. In practice a certain amount of trial and error is necessary to establish the correct time and temperature. It is always a good idea to check the crust about halfway through the recipe time. If it is already highly colored you should turn down the heat.

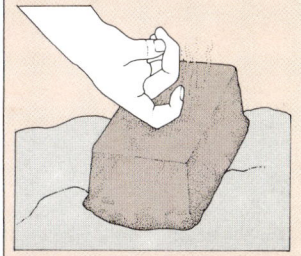

NB: *If the loaf comes out of the tin easily and has a hollow sound when tapped on the bottom your bread is done.*

BASIC TECHNIQUES

RISING TECHNIQUES

Bulk fermentation
This is the stage which follows mixing and which allows the yeast to develop the gluten in the flour. Low gluten flour, such as wholewheat, requires little bulk fermentation.

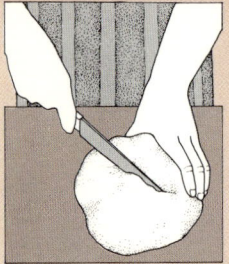

Intermediate rising
After punching down and kneading, the dough is allowed a few minutes to recover before cutting and moulding. This is the intermediate rising.

Final rising
This is the true rising stage – when the dough is allowed to reach its final size and shape. At this stage it will be in its tin or on the baking sheet ready for the oven.

Rising

There are three stages in raising dough, the first of which is known as *bulk fermentation*. This is the period during which the dough is rested immediately after mixing, thus allowing the yeast to develop the gluten in the flour by stretching the elasticity of the dough through the production of carbon dioxide gasses. This stage can last anything from $\frac{1}{2}$ hr to 24 hrs depending on the proportion of yeast to flour. During this period the dough should be re-kneaded (punched down) to expel the carbon dioxide and incorporate oxygen as well as to help with the development process.

The second, and shortest, raising period is the rest given to the dough piece after cutting and weighing and before final moulding. This is known as the *intermediate rising*.

The *final rising* is the process the bread goes through immediately prior to baking. Raising the prepared bread before it is set and baked in the oven allows the yeast to stretch the dough to the final shape and size at which it will produce the best possible textures and eating qualities. To provide the best condition for this process it is necessary to keep the dough at the optimum temperature for the yeast to do its work; at the same time, the dough should not be allowed to scum because this will retard the rising process and reduce the volume of the baked loaf. Scumming will occur if the dough is left in a warm dry atmosphere or in a drafty place. In other words, moisture should be introduced into the warm atmosphere in which the dough is rising. A steamy room or cupboard, is the ideal medium for final rising. However, in many domestic kitchens these conditions are not possible, so a bathroom with hot water filling a bath can often be an ideal alternative. The only other possibility is to cover the bread tins with a clean damp cloth or plastic sheet. A word of warning though: do not allow the cloth or plastic to come into contact with the dough because they will stick together, and pulling them apart will result in the dough falling back and the whole process of moulding and raising will have to be gone through again.

At any stage of the raising process your dough may take longer to rise than the recipes indicate. Provided that the atmosphere is not too dry, there is no need to worry.

IS RISING COMPLETE?

In the case of tin bread the loaf should be just above the top of the loaf tin with the crown of the loaf nicely risen. If your dough is in the shape of cakes, small buns etc. the bulk of the dough should have approximately doubled, if you then press your finger very lightly into the side of the dough and the impression remains for some time, the dough is ready to bake.

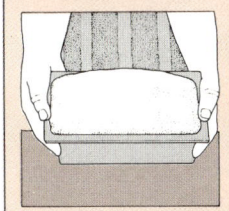

Tin bread
Be careful not to let the dough rise too much above the tin. If you do, the crust may split away from the loaf and the texture may be impaired.

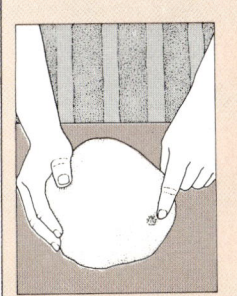

Testing the dough
If, when you press your finger into the dough, the impression remains for some time, the rising has slowed down and the loaf is ready to bake. This is a good test for any loaf which is not in a tin.

MOULDING AND KNEADING

Mixing various raw materials into bread dough can be done fairly easily by anyone who can follow a good recipe. The skill in breadmaking (and the most difficult process to learn) lies in the kneading and moulding of the dough. To learn the skills of moulding from the written word is not easy even when illustrations are included in the instructions and it is a very good idea for the aspiring baker to make up an unleavened dough on which to practice and develop his skills. To make up a yeastless dough, simply mix 270g (2 cups) water and 450g (4 cups) flour into a dough. This dough can then be kept in the refrigerator for quite some time before natural fermentation makes the dough sour.

The most important parts of the hands, when being used for kneading, are the heel and the knuckles and not, as most novice breadmakers seem to think, the palm and the fingers. The dough should always be handled firmly as hard treatment helps to develop the gluten in the flour which, of course, improves the final loaf.

How to knead dough

1. When the dough has been mixed it should be gathered into a piece and the baking surface lightly floured.

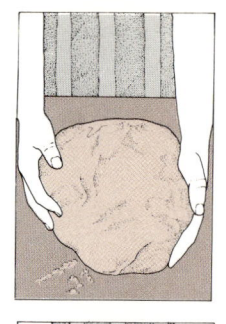

2. Using the heel of the hand to push the dough at its base, and using the palm and fingers as a retaining guide on top of the dough, form the dough piece into a rounded oblong shape.

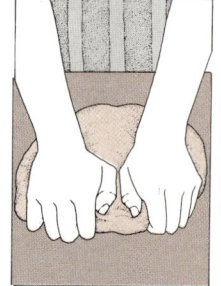

3. Using the knuckles, firmly press the dough into a square shape which gives access for both hands to begin the tearing process.

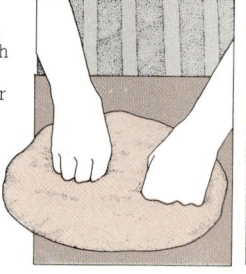

4. Grip the nearer end of the dough with the palm and fingers of one hand and with the heel of the other hand pull and stretch the other end of the dough piece away from the fingers until its stretching limit is reached.

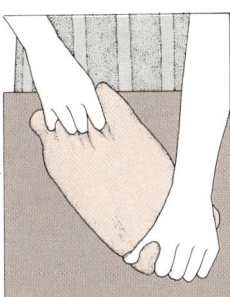

5. Again starting with the heel of the hand roll the dough piece back upon itself until it is completely rolled up and forms a basic loaf shape.

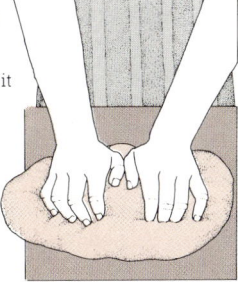

6. Turn the dough through 90° and repeat the process from step 3. Keep on repeating this kneading until a smooth silky dough has been developed.

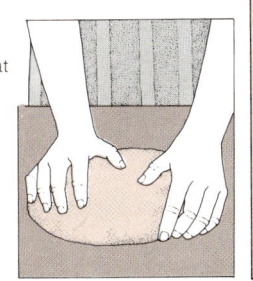

HOW TO MOULD DOUGH

After the dough has undergone bulk fermentation repeat the kneading process for three turns of the dough – this will give you an ideal shape for tin bread. If you require the dough to be balled up then just give the dough one round of kneading, then starting with the side of the hand in a firm semi-circular movement, bring the dough round into a ball shape using the little finger to tuck in the tail of dough at the bottom. Continue this process until a round, smooth ball of dough is achieved.

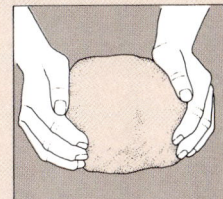

Tin loaves
If, as you knead, you turn the dough through 90° three times, you will find that a rectangular shape is formed. With a little adjustment it will be suitable for placing in the tin.

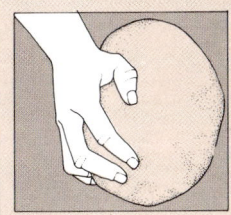

Round loaves
When moulding round loaves, be sure to keep the shape even by tucking underneath the loose ends of dough. You can do this with your little finger as you turn the dough around.

BASIC TECHNIQUES

BASIC RECIPE 1

Ingredients

1.35kg	flour	12 cups
26g	salt	1½ Tbs
30g	yeast	2 Tbs
30g	fat *white fat, lard, oil, or unsalted butter*	2 Tbs
15g	sugar	1 Tbs
¾ litre	water *at approx 31°C, (90°F)*	3 cups

Straight dough
Method 1

Sift the flour and salt together, rub in the fat until it is thoroughly dispersed in the flour and make a well in the mixture.

Dissolve the sugar in the water, crumble the yeast into the liquid and stir with a whisk or fork until the yeast is dispersed evenly with no lumps.

Pour the water/yeast mixture into the well. Gradually draw the flour into the water until a soft sticky dough is achieved. Using both hands, knead and tear the dough until it has a smooth silky feel to it. This will take about 10 to 15 minutes.

Cover the dough with a damp cloth and leave in a warm, draft-free place to rise. After 20 minutes, punch down the dough, then again cover the dough with the cloth and leave for a further 20 minutes.

During this time the oven may be pre-heated to 230°C (450°F), and the tins greased.

The dough is now ready to use. Knead it until the air is expelled, and cut the dough to the required size. Allow to 'recover' for 3 to 4 minutes then mould into shape and place the pieces into slightly warmed tins covering them with a cloth. If you are working in a warm steamy kitchen the conditions are ideal for raising your bread. If not, try to ensure that no drafts can reach your bread and form a scum on the surface.

When your loaves have nearly reached the top of the tins, remove the cloth to ensure that the dough does not stick to it. Allow the dough to rise until the crest of the domed top of the loaf is about an inch higher than the tin. Taking care not to knock the tins or stick your fingers into the dough, place the tins into the oven and leave for 20 minutes before checking your bread. If the loaves have a high top color (if they are browning rapidly) turn the oven down to 180°C (350°F) and leave for a further 20 to 25 minutes until baked. Remove the bread from the oven, and then from the tins, placing the baked loaves on wire cooling racks to allow the air to circulate around the bread.

● Bread is best if cooled rapidly, so it may be advisable to remove the baked loaves from the kitchen to a cooler room. If you want the crust to remain crisp for a reasonable length of time, do not wrap the loaf or put into a storage tin until the day after baking.

TIPS AND TECHNIQUES

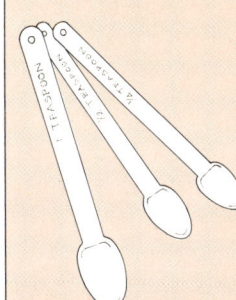

◀ **Correct measurement**
Quantities of salt, sugar, liquid, fats, etc. should be accurately measured because they can have considerable effect upon the bread. A set of measuring spoons is essential.

◀ **The importance of salt**
Salt is one of the most critical ingredients of bread. Without it, bread can be almost tasteless; with too much, it will be slow to rise and may have a hard crust.

◀ **Mixing**
Dough is best mixed by hand or mixer. Mixing with forks or other implements is not recommended. Mixing is not complete until individual ingredients cannot be distinguished.

BASIC RECIPE 2

Ferment:

450g	flour	4 cups
30g	yeast	2 Tbs
15g	sugar	1 Tbs
¾ litre	water *at approx 32°C (90°F)*	3 cups

Dough:

900g	flour	8 cups
26g	salt	1½ Tbs
30g	fat	2 Tbs

Ferment and dough
Method 2

This method of dough making can be used in various forms. The first method described is the most basic and can be used in all forms of breadmaking when the straight dough method (I) is either not suitable for the dough required or wrong for the conditions in which it is made.

For this method, make sure you use a container which will allow the ferment to double in volume.

Stir the sugar into the water until dissolved. Crumble the yeast into the liquid and mix in well. Add the flour and mix with the yeast/water mixture until it is of an even consistency and contains no lumps.

Set the bowl aside until the ferment has doubled in volume or until bubbles appear on the top (approx. 20 to 30 minutes).

Rub the fat and the salt into the flour until it has an even crumbly consistency and then make a well in the middle of the mixture.

When the ferment is ready, pour it into the well of flour and draw the flour evenly into the center (this prevents the liquid from flowing all over the baking table). When a dough is formed any further water or flour may be added.

The dough should now be kneaded well as described in Method I.

When you have achieved a smooth silky dough, cover it with a damp cloth or a sheet of plastic for half an hour. Punch the dough down and then cut and mould into the shapes required.

Let rise and bake your bread as in Method I.

Notes on temperature

In domestic ovens, whether heated by gas or electricity, temperatures will be higher at the top of the oven than at the bottom. The temperatures indicated in the recipes and methods described in this book refer to the center of the oven and assume that the oven functions efficiently, with no variations of temperature. However, it is frequently found that some ovens will, when set to a chosen mark, bake faster or slower than the rate assumed by the recipe. The only way to be sure that you are not baking your loaves too fast is to check them half-way through the recipe time and reduce the heat if they are browning too rapidly. Baking too slowly is not altogether desirable, but is unlikely to be disastrous.

TIPS AND TECHNIQUES

◀ Mixing the ferment
This method is designed to encourage a faster fermentation. What you are doing during the mixing is to force a lot of air into a mixture which contains as few yeast inhibitors as possible.

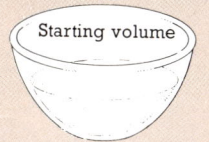

Starting volume

Leave until doubled

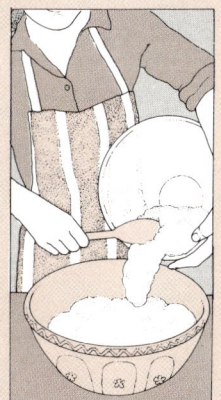

◀ Making the dough
In this stage of the process, the ferment takes the place of the liquid ingredients in the first method of dough making. Mixing and kneading will be the same.

BASIC RECIPE 3

Ferment:

675g	flour	6 cups
60g	yeast	4 Tbs
30g	sugar	2 Tbs
¾ litre	water *at approx* 32°C (90°F)	3 cups

Dough:

675g	flour	6 cups
26g	salt	1½ Tbs
30g	fat	2 Tbs

Flying sponge
Method 3

In the baking trade this is known as an emergency dough making method – when bread has to be produced quickly with as little bulk fermentation time as possible. It is more suitable for an electric mixer than for hand mixing.

Using a recipe very similar to the one used in Methods I and II:

The ferment
Make up the ferment as in Method II but set aside for 15 minutes only.

The dough
Mix to a crumbly consistency in a mixer on low speed.

When the ferment or sponge is ready, add to the dough and mix well.

When the dough is smooth, cover for 15 minutes, punch down and cut to the required size and mould.

Let rise and bake as before.

●

Using milk in dough
The dough used for this recipe is ideal for all forms of twisting and plaiting, but it can be used as the basis for any milk enriched loaf. Milk is almost as important as water in dough making. The fat in the milk helps to improve the texture of the loaf and certainly increases its keeping qualities. Milk produces a soft crust on any bread in which it is used

TRADITIONAL

1. Basic ingredients and recipe
2. Bloomer loaf
3. Cottage loaf
4. Coburg
5. Round
6. Oven bottom cakes
7. Brown bread
8. Wholewheat bread

Traditional loaves
This section is basically concerned with the shape and style of loaves. Using the methods described in the previous section, we show how to make a variety of loaves which have been baked and sold for generations – even centuries.

Although wholewheat bread and brown loaves have to be made with the appropriate flours, and the others are usually made with white flour, there is no reason why the shapes should not be achieved with any flour you care to use. Those that require cuts in the crust will work best, however, if made with white flour – or with a substantial proportion of white flour.

Traditional bread—Basic recipe

Ingredients:

450g	flour	4 cups
7g	salt	1 Tsp
7g	sugar	1 Tsp
15g	yeast	1 Tbs
¼ litre	**water** or *half water and half milk*	1 cup

Method:

Make the dough as described in Methods I or II, giving a bulk fermentation of 1 hour punching down at 30 minutes and at the end of fermentation.

The only variation in this type of loaf is the shape. However, this does not mean to say that each loaf will taste the same. The rising and baking of the breads can vary both the texture and flavor of the eventual loaf even if the same recipe is used. The whole of baking, be it bread or confectionary, relies on the air as the catalyst which makes basically similar raw materials into myriad different products. The shapes given to various bread doughs have an enormous relevance to the 'aeration' factor. Therefore, it becomes easier to appreciate that a different shaped loaf can become a different tasting loaf, so it is important that you should become acquainted with moulding bread into many diverse shapes, just as it is important to be able to use and vary recipes to your particular need.

Making traditional shapes

This section is devoted to the moulding or shaping of bread. The recipe is suitable to all breads in this section, but you may and should vary the recipe and use as many different variations as may be fitting for this particular type of bread.

You may note that the sugar and milk content in recipes for the more traditional loaf are rather low. This is mainly because this type of bread is usually required to be 'crusty' and both milk and sugar soften the outer crust of bread in which they are more liberally used.

The dough from the recipe given can be used as a whole or split into two pieces as desired. The methods given are for the whole dough but, if smaller loaves are preferred, halve all the quantities given and make into two halves of one type or two small loaves of different shape.

Bloomer loaf

Mould the whole dough piece into a ball, then immediately mould the ball into a long loaf shape (about half as long again as the normal loaf).

Place the dough on a pre-greased baking sheet and with a sharp knife make four or five diagonal cuts across the top of the loaf's surface.

Prove for 30 to 40 minutes and bake in a hot oven at 230°C (450°F) for 35 to 45 minutes.

Cottage loaf

Split the dough into two pieces one weighing 550g ((20oz) and one 180g (6oz). Mould both pieces round and flatten them slightly with the hand.

Place the smaller piece on top of the larger making sure that it is in the center – otherwise the small piece will fall off the base when baking and spoil the shape of the loaf.

Place the loaf on a pre-greased baking sheet and with the forefinger make a hole right through the center of both pieces until you reach the tin.

Let rise for about 30 to 40 minutes, or until ready, and bake in a hot oven at 230°C (450°F) for 40 to 50 minutes.

TRADITIONAL LOAVES

TRADITIONAL LOAVES

Coburg loaf 4

This is suitable for two smaller loaves.
Split the dough into two equal parts and mould round.

Place each round dough piece into a pre-greased round cake tin approximately 12.5cm × 2.5cm deep (5in × 1in).

With a sharp knife make a cross-shaped incision (about 3.5cm/1½in) in the top of the loaf.

Let rise for 45 to 60 minutes and bake at 230°C (450°F) for 40 to 50 minutes.

Round loaf 5

From the whole dough piece, take a 60g (¼ cup) piece and mould round. Mould the rest of the dough into a loaf shape and place on a pre-greased baking sheet.

With your hands, roll the small dough ball into a strip approx 23cm (9in) long and place it lengthways across the center of the loaf, making sure that the ends are tucked underneath the large dough piece.

Wash the dough with egg and sprinkle poppy seed along the thin strip.

Let rise for 40 to 50 minutes and bake at 220°C (425°F) for 45 to 50 minutes.

Oven bottom cakes 6

Split the dough into two pieces and mould them into balls. Cover with a cloth and let them rest for 10 minutes.

Pin each piece out into 23cm (9in) circles and make a hole in the center of each with the forefinger.

You will need a baking sheet for each cake and each sheet should be covered with either raw semolina or ground rice flour. If you have neither of these materials just grease the tins well. Place each cake on a tin and let rise for 20 to 30 minutes.

When risen, put the cakes in a hot oven 230°C (450°F) and leave for 5 to 10 minutes. When the bottoms of the cakes are part baked, take the tins out of the oven and turn each cake over before putting back into the oven for a further 10 minutes.

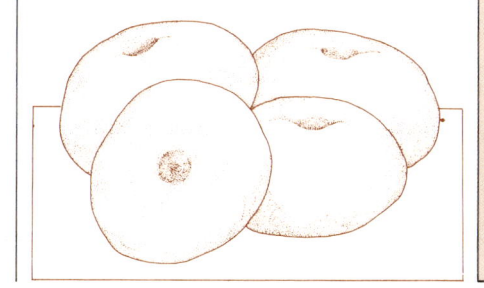

CUTTING THE CRUST

You will have noticed that a number of traditional loaves and loaf shapes incorporate cuts in the crust. When this is done, the total area of crust is increased as the dough rises and pushes through the slits or cuts. The crust in the cut area is slightly different to the smooth and brittle crust on an uncut loaf, being coarser and somewhat richer in flavor.

There is no secret method of successful cutting – if the dough is good and full of 'spring' it should take cuts well. Always make deep incisions with a sharp implement and make them smoothly – do not agitate the dough as you cut.

With practice, quite elaborate patterns can be achieved with cutting, but you must be sure that your dough is good enough to take them.

Cutting the dough

TRADITIONAL LOAVES

Brown bread

Ingredients:

900g	rye flour	8 cups
26g	salt	1½ Tbs
30g	fat	2 Tbs
30g	syrup	2 Tbs
30g	liquid malt extract	2 Tbs
45g	yeast	3 Tbs
0.6 litre	**water** *lukewarm*	2 cups

Brown bread recipes can vary according to the type of brown flour available; some brown flours have salt added and some have high malt ratios. On many bags of brown flour the millers will have given their own recommended recipe. The recipe given here is a general brown bread one and can be adapted to the flour used. This recipe is also suitable for Granary bread.

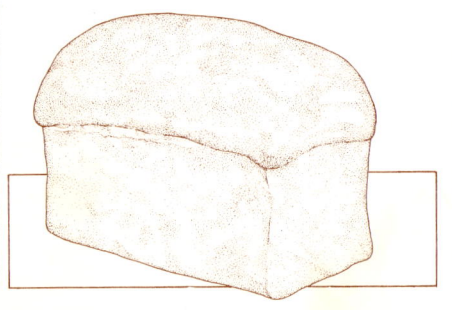

Rub the fat and salt into the flour and make a well.

Stir the malt and syrup into the water, crumble in the yeast and mix until dissolved.

Pour the liquid into the flour well and draw in the flour to form a dough.

Knead the dough for 5 to 7 minutes and let it rest for 30 minutes punching down once half-way through fermentation.

After bulk fermentation is completed, punch down the dough again and cut to required size.

Mould either into a loaf shape, or round into a ball if that is what you want.

Let rise for 30 to 40 minutes allowing the dough to reach the size you require from the baked loaf (brown flour has very little 'oven spring' and will not increase much in volume while baking).

Bake at 220°C (425°F) for about 40 to 45 minutes.

When baked, remove from tins immediately and cool on racks. This recipe is suitable for almost any shape or size of loaf. All the traditional loaves can be made from brown flours.

Wholewheat bread

Ingredients:

450g	stone ground, wholewheat flour	4 cups
7g	salt	1 Tsp
30g	corn oil	2 Tbs
15g	yeast	1 Tbs
15g	sugar	1 Tbs
¼ litre	water *32°C (90°F)*	1 cup

An electric mixer is recommended for this because of the stickiness of the recipe.

This recipe goes straight from mixing to moulding and involves very little rising and kneading

Wholewheat flour is rather unstable and does not respond well to handling.

Mix the flour, oil and salt together until well dispersed.

Stir the sugar into the warm water and then crumble in the yeast. Whisk until dissolved.

Add the yeast/water mixture to the flour and mix on a slow speed for 10 minutes. This dough requires a fairly long mixing time, not for the usual reason of developing the gluten (this is a very low gluten flour), but because the flour grain is hard and husky and it takes quite a long time to absorb the water. After five minutes mixing, check the dough to see if the water has been absorbed and add any more if required – because a fairly soft dough is needed.

As soon as the dough is mixed, take it out of the mixer and mould into a loaf shape immediately.

Put into a well greased 450g (4 cups) loaf tin.

Allow to rise for 15 minutes only, then bake in a moderately hot oven at 220°C (425°F) for 45 minutes.

When baked, remove from the tin and put on a wire to cool. Wholewheat flour can be used for traditional shapes, but the dough will not open out well if cuts are required.

TRADITIONAL LOAVES

SPECIAL RECIPES

1. Croissants
2. Brioche
3. Muffins
4. Crumpets

Special recipes
The recipes contained within this part of the book are different from the others in that their methods of preparation are more complex, or they require a different baking technique. Croissants call for a very repetitive preparation, but they are not really difficult to make. Brioches require almost 24 hours to make, but the amount of work involved is not extensive.
Crumpets and English muffins are both cooked on a griddle and are very rewarding, once the technique has been mastered.

How to make croissants

At first glance, making croissants may appear to be a rather daunting job but, although repetitive, the recipe is really quite simple and not so time consuming as it looks. Freshly baked croissants can be so rewarding that every baker should try them at least once!

Ingredients:

450g	flour	4 cups
60g	sugar	¼ cup
¼ litre	water or milk *lukewarm*	1 cup
30g	yeast	2 Tbs
30g	butter	2 Tbs
7g	salt	1 Tsp
225g	butter *well chilled*	8oz

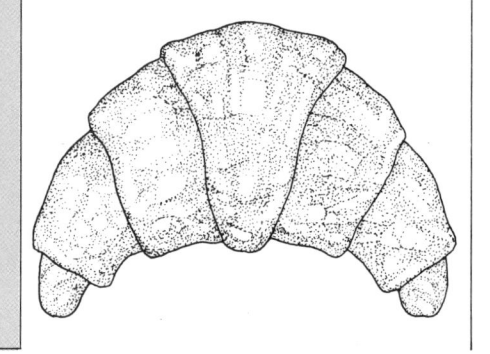

Method:

1. *Make the dough in the usual way and let it rest for 25 minutes.*

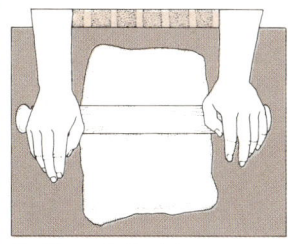

2. *The chilled butter must be rolled out into a 2cm (¾in) thick square approximately 23cm × 23cm (9in × 9in). An easy way of doing this is to place the butter between two sheets of greaseproof or wax paper before rolling out with a pin. As soon as the butter is rolled to shape, put it back in the fridge until required.*

3. *After the bulk fermentation is complete knock the dough back and mould into a ball. Let it rest for 10 minutes.*

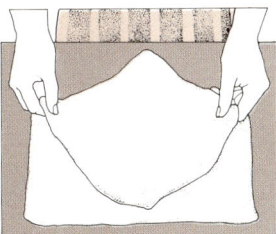

4. *Roll the dough piece out into a square 30cm × 30cm (12in × 12in). Take the butter from the refrigerator and place diagonally across the center of the dough.*

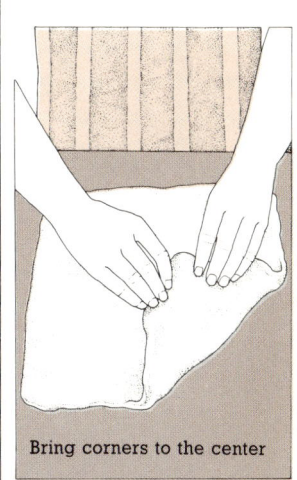

Bring corners to the center

5. *Bring the corners of the dough to meet in the center making sure that all the butter is covered. Put the square in the refrigerator for 10 minutes.*

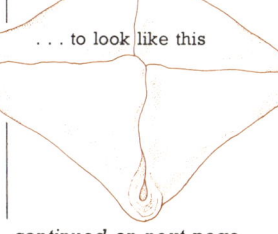

. . . to look like this

continued on next page

SPECIAL RECIPES

How to make croissants
continued

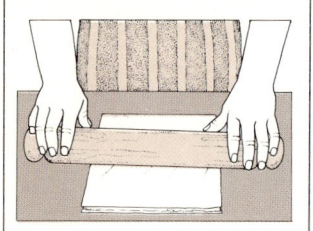

Roll dough into an oblong

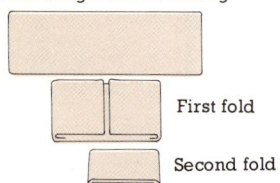

First fold

Second fold

6. *After resting, take the dough square and place it folded side down onto the table. Roll the dough into an oblong about 50cm × 25cm (20in × 10in). Take both ends of the dough and fold them so that they nearly meet in the center of the piece. Then fold one half over the other.*
Replace the folded dough in the refrigerator for 30 minutes.

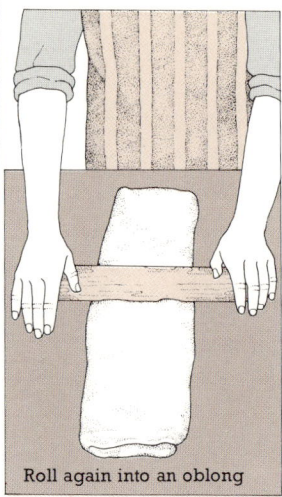

Roll again into an oblong

7. *After resting, remove the dough from the refrigerator and once more pin out into an oblong 50cm × 25cm (20in × 10in). Repeat the folding process and again place the piece in the refrigerator for a further 30 minutes. Take the dough piece out and roll into an oblong strip about 6mm ($\frac{1}{4}$in) thick and 12.5cm (5in) deep.*

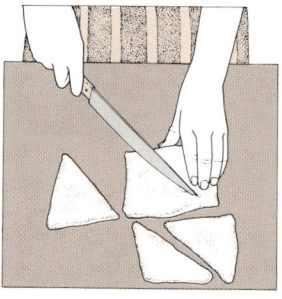

8. *Cut the dough into 12.5cm (5in) squares and then cut each square diagonally in half.*

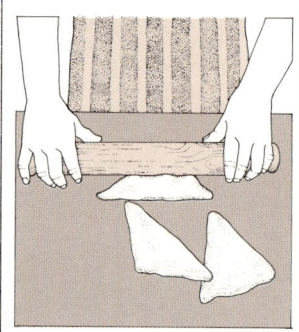

9. *Gently roll each triangle out so that its area is increased by a third.*

10. Roll each piece up from the base of the triangle and seal the ends with a little eggwash.

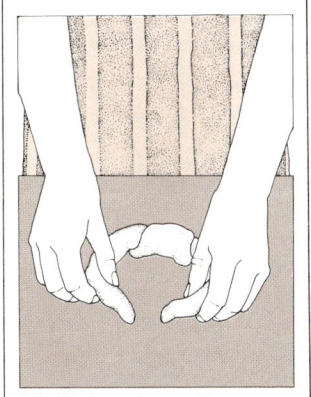

11. Bring the roll round so that the ends meet and press them lightly together to form a crescent.

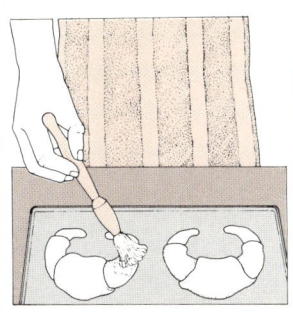

12. Eggwash the croissants and place them on a pre-greased baking sheet to rise for 30 minutes. Bake in a hot oven at 220°C (425°F) for 15 minutes or until golden brown in color.

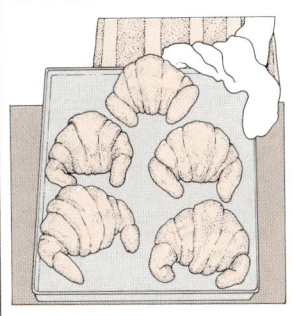

FURTHER SUGGESTIONS

Croissants jambons
Smoked ham is a delicious addition to croissants – one that almost turns them into a meal. For this version of croissants the sugar in the dough should be reduced to 7g (1 Tsp). Just before rolling the dough into its characteristic shape, lay a slice of ham on the dough. Roll the croissant with the ham inside and leave to rise.

Petits pains au chocolats
Using croissant dough or plain bread dough, make small rectangles and cover them with 15g (1 Tbs) melted plain chocolate. Roll up the dough and leave to rise in the usual way.

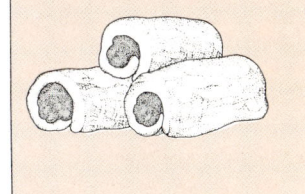

SPECIAL RECIPES

Brioches

The brioche is a French dough bun and can be made either as a large dough bun, several individual buns or a ring.

They can be baked in specially fluted brioche tins or on a baking sheet.

The brioche is a versatile bread; with its center cut out and the cavity filled with soft fruit such as strawberries, raspberries or black cherries, and topped with whipped cream, it makes a delicious dessert. At coffee time, try a warm brioche with homemade strawberry jam to bring an air of luxury to any rainy morning. Even if your brioche goes stale it will make the most delicious toast you have ever tasted.

Making brioches is much more complex than most breads and it is not the best recipe for a novice baker to begin with. When a little skill and experience has been developed, however, your craftsmanship will be well rewarded.

Ingredients:

280g	flour	2 cups
	two eggs	
2g	salt	¼ Tsp
100g	butter	3½oz
15g	yeast	1 Tbs
30g	sugar	2 Tbs
85ml	water *cool*	⅓ cup

TYPES OF BRIOCHE

Filled brioches
Try brioches filled with fresh fruit and cream.

Brioche en couronne
A traditional brioche shape – baked without a mould.

Ring type

Fluted

Brioche tins

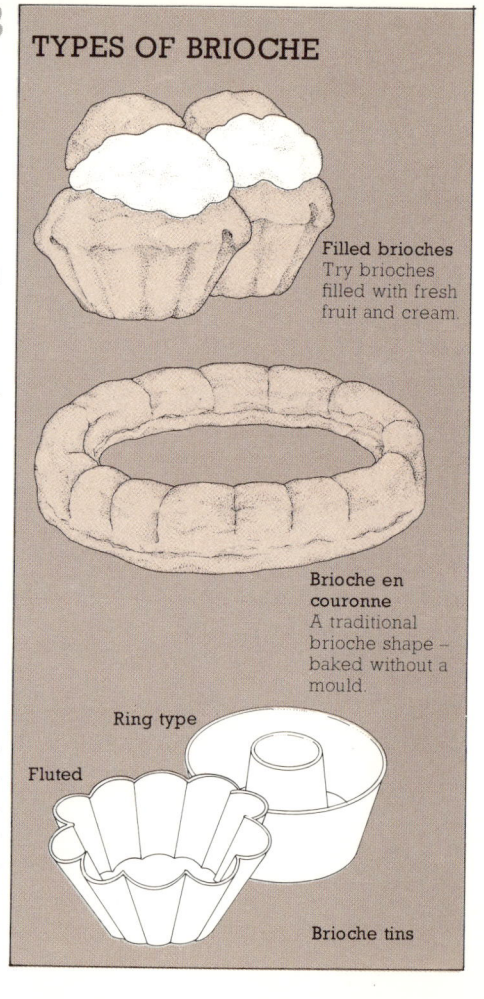

How to make brioche

1. Stir the sugar into the water, crumble in the yeast and mix until dispersed.

2. Take half of the flour and mix it lightly into the water. Do not try to make a smooth dough because what you require here is a stiff lumpy ferment.

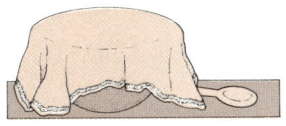

3. Cover the bowl with a cloth and set aside to allow the ferment to double in size (approx 60 minutes).

4. Soften the butter slightly by beating it, then very carefully rub in the rest of the flour. When you have achieved the consistency of a crumble stop mixing, otherwise the flour and butter will form a paste which will be useless. Then make a well.

5. Add the salt to the eggs and mix them together. Do not whisk the eggs, just stir until homogenized.

6. When the ferment is ready add the eggs to it and, with the fingers, amalgamate the egg and salt into the ferment.

Continued on next page

SPECIAL RECIPES

How to make brioche
continued

7. Pour the ferment into the well and draw in the flour to make a soft sticky dough.

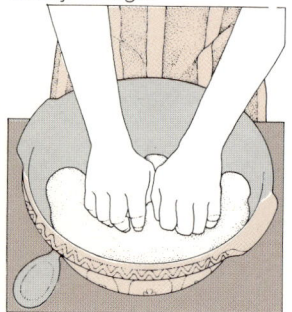

8. With the heel of the hand, knead and tear the dough for about 10 to 12 minutes.

9. Put the dough into a floured bowl and cover. Place the bowl in the refrigerator and leave overnight (at least 12 hours).

10. After bulk fermentation punch down the dough and break off about one quarter of it. Make each piece into a ball and let them rest for 5 minutes.

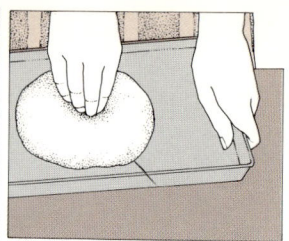

11. Place the large ball onto a pre-greased baking sheet or in a brioche tin and with three fingers make a large hole in the center of the dough.

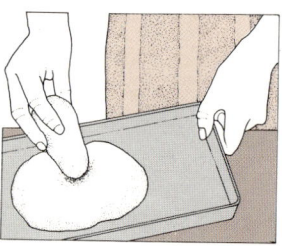

12. With the palm of the hand roll one end of the small dough piece into a tail, about the size of the indentation in the large dough piece. Put the small dough piece on top of the large one, so that the tail fits into the hole, and eggwash.

SPECIAL RECIPES

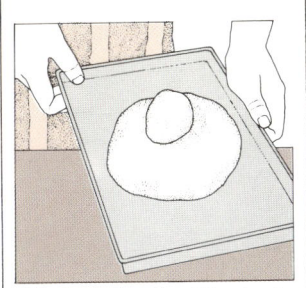

13. *Let rise for 20 minutes and bake in a hot oven at 220°C (425°F) for 15 minutes.*

Specialties ▶
Brioches are the delicacies of yeast baking. They come in many shapes and sizes, but all are subtly flavored. By contrast, crumpets and English muffins are very down-to-earth, but no less delicious for that.

English muffins

Ingredients

570g	bread flour	4¼ cups
15g	salt	1 Tbs
22g	yeast	1½ Tbs
7g	sugar	1 Tsp
60g	butter	2oz
0.6 litre	water *(lukewarm)*	2 cups

Rub the fat and salt into the flour until a fine crumbly consistency is achieved and make a well.

Stir the sugar into the water and dissolve the yeast in it.

Pour the liquor into the flour well, draw in the flour and mix very well.

Cover and leave in a draft-free place for 1½ hours punching down after 1 hour.

Cut into 85g to 115g (6–8 Tbs) pieces and mould round – this will not be easy because the dough is very soft and sticky.

Liberally sprinkle a board with ground rice and leave the muffins on it for 20 to 30 minutes.

Lightly grease muffin rings – any open ended metal ring with a 7.5cm (3in) diameter and a depth of 2.5cm 3.5cm (1in to 1½in). The original muffin was square in shape and a 7.5cm × 7.5cm (3in × 3in) square tin can also be used if available.

Immediately before baking place the rings on the clean griddle. (NB: Do not allow the griddle to reach too high a temperature.) Then carefully place the muffins into the rings on the griddle. As soon as the bases of the muffins are colored, turn them over and bake the other side similarly.

●

Muffins are an essentially English institution, though similar griddle cakes are found in many parts of the world. Recipes differ considerably from region to region – as does the general understanding of the meaning of 'muffin'.

Crumpets

Ingredients

450g	flour	4 cups
15g	yeast	1 Tbs
	pinch of sugar	
	pinch of salt	
200ml	milk *warm*	1 cup
200ml	water *warm*	1 cup
	pinch of baking soda	

Pour the warm milk and water into a large bowl into which the sugar, salt and yeast are dissolved. Stirring continuously with a whisk, slowly add the flour until a smooth batter is obtained.

Set the bowl aside in a warm draft-free place for 1½ hours or until the ferment has risen and fallen again.

Dissolve a pinch of baking soda into 60g (¼ cup) water and stir well into the ferment. Leave for 10–15 minutes.

Place lightly greased hoops onto the well cleaned griddle and ladle the crumpet mixture into them until about two-thirds full.

When the batter has 'holed' the crumpets should be turned with a palette knife and left just long enough for the top to begin to color.

There is enough mixture in this recipe for about 18 crumpets, so if the rings have to be used several times make sure they are re-greased every second application.

If you have no suitable hoops to use as crumpet rings then you may pour enough of the mixture directly onto the griddle to form a 5in circle of batter and cook in the same way. The end result from this method being known as pikelets.

Crumpets are not too difficult to make and, once you have achieved a successful batch at home, you will find that there is little comparison, except in appearance, with the store variety.

TWISTS & PLAITS

1. Four piece loaf
2. Three strand plait
3. Corkscrew
4. Coil
5. Twist

Twisted and plaited loaves
Everyone likes unusual and attractively shaped loaves – and not just for special occasions. Plaits, twists and coils with glistening brown crusts lend something special to any table, and they are very popular with children.

The dough described for the four piece loaf can be used as the basis for many variations on the shapes described on the next few pages, but elaborate festival loaves should be made with a water based dough.

Four piece loaf

Ingredients:

900g	flour	8 cups
30g	sugar	2 Tbs
15g	salt	1 Tbs
30g	margarine or oil	2 Tbs
	one egg	
400ml	milk *warm*	1¾ cups
30g	yeast	2 Tbs

Rub the fat into the flour and salt. Stir the sugar into the lukewarm milk, crumble in the yeast and stir until dissolved. Add the milk mixture and the egg to the flour and mix well.

This bread ferments a little quicker than a basic dough and bulk fermentation time should be reduced. The dough is also very suitable for the use of vitamin 'C' tablets because it is very springy and awkward to handle after a long bulk fermentation.

When the dough is ready, cut into three 450g (4 cups) loaves or one 900g (8 cups) loaf plus one 450g (4 cups) loaf.

For the larger loaf, divide the dough into four pieces: 2 at 340g (3 cups) and 2 at 115g (1 cup). For the smaller loaf, halve these weights.

First mould the two large pieces into balls and place them together. Then mould the two smaller pieces into balls and put one at each side of the larger ones.

Put the pieces into the appropriate tin and carefully eggwash the center of the loaf, taking care not to allow the egg to go too near the sides or, when the loaf is rising, the egg will stick to the tin.

After rising the loaf very carefully, eggwash the top for a second time using only light strokes of the brush so as not to punch down the dough.

If you enjoy a little added flavor and color, sprinkle the top of the loaf with some poppy seeds.

Bake at 220°C (425°F).

PLAITED LOAVES

The shapes described on the next few pages are all easy to make but, once you have mastered the skills of shaping them, you will be able to go on to much more elaborate shapes.

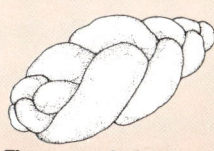

Three strand plait
Similar to the Vienna loaf; can be 450g (4 cups) or larger. It is usually covered with poppy seeds.

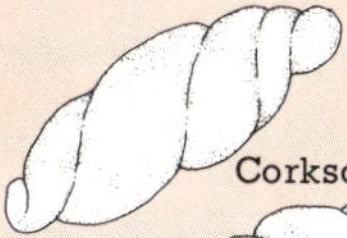

Three strand plait

Corkscrew
A very satisfying shape to make, but it can turn out to look very like a plait.

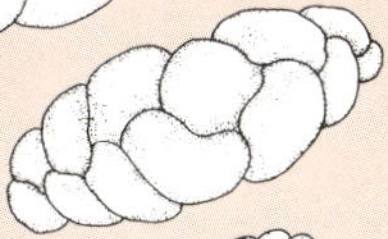

Corkscrew

Twist
A variation of plaiting which can be done with small or large pieces of dough.

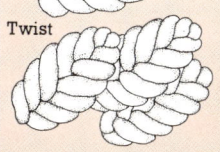

Twist

Small plaits
Roll-sized versions of the three strand plait.

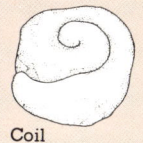

Small plaits

Coil
A simple, but attractive, alternative to the usual roll shapes.

Coil

TWISTS AND PLAITS

How to make a three strand plait

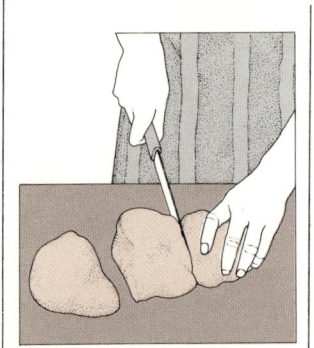

TWISTS AND PLAITS

1. Measure a 450g (4 cups) dough piece and split into three equal pieces and mould into balls.

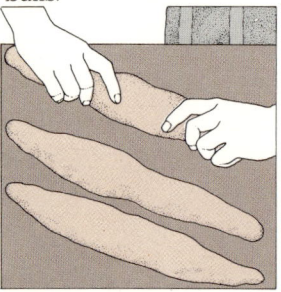

2. Mould each piece into 30cm (12in) long strands each being narrower at the ends than in the center.

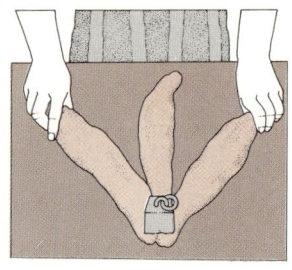

3. Place the strands into a fan shape with the narrow closed ends placed over each other and a weight put on the top to hold these ends together.

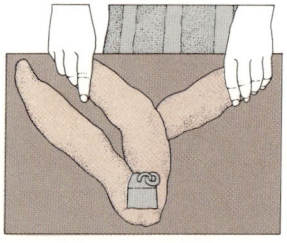

4. Take the dough piece on the left and lift it over the center piece, at the same time pulling the center strand out to the left.

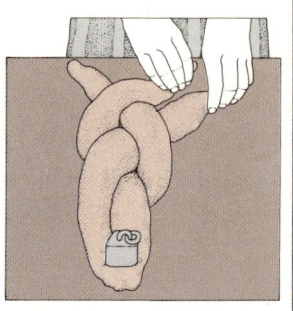

5. Repeat the process using the right strand, and so on until the end of the plait, then pinch the ends together.

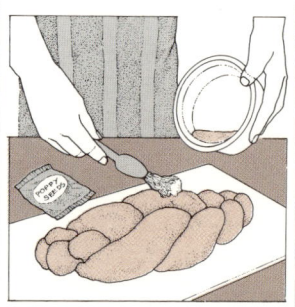

6. Eggwash the plait well and sprinkle with poppy seeds.

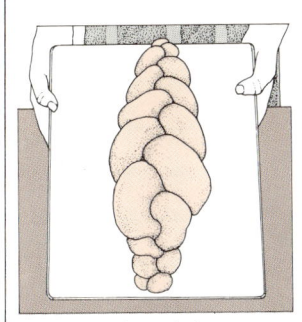

7. *Place the plait on a baking sheet and prove and bake as before.*

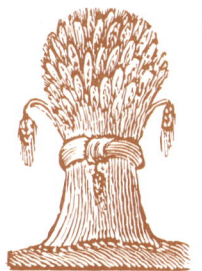

Roll shapes ▶
The basic dough used for white or wholewheat breads can also be used for making the rolls shown here. They are ideal for serving with soups or snacks.

TWISTS AND PLAITS

TWISTS AND PLAITS

How to make a corkscrew 3

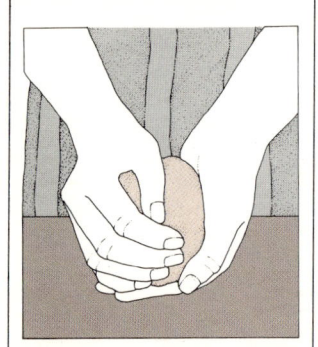

1. Take an 85g (6 Tbs) dough piece and mould into a ball. Let it rest 5 minutes.

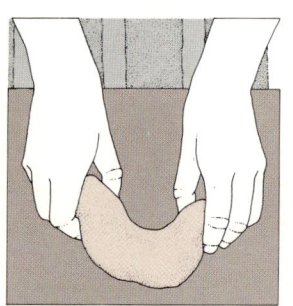

2. Roll the dough out into a strand approximately 18cm (7in) long and fold the strand into half.

3. Twist the two halves together, nipping the ends.

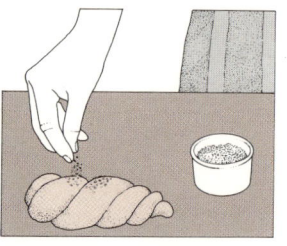

4. Eggwash and sprinkle poppy seeds lightly on the top. Place on a pre-greased baking sheet and let rise. Bake at 220°C (425°F) for 10 to 15 minutes.

Plaits 4

Take a 115g (8 Tbs) dough piece and split into three equal pieces moulding each piece into a ball.

Mould each piece into a 30cm (12in) long strand, as you would for a three strand plait.

Place the dough into a fan shape and follow exactly the same procedure for plaiting as described for the three strand plait (page 64).

Eggwash the plait and sprinkle with poppy seeds.

Bake at 220°C (425°F) for 15 to 20 minutes.

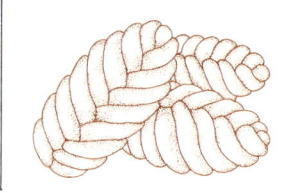

How to make a twist

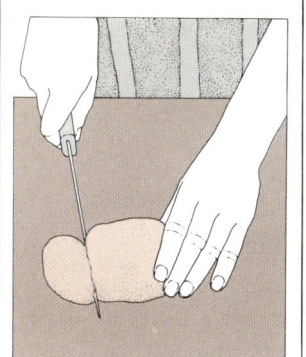

1. *Take a 115g (8 Tbs) dough piece and split into three equal parts.*

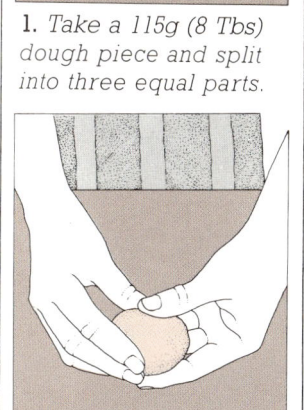

2. *Mould into balls and let them rest for 5 to 10 minutes.*

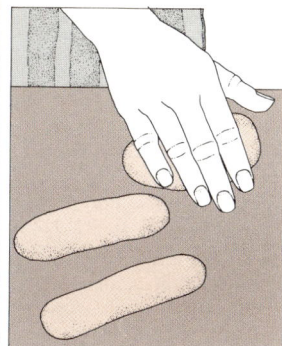

3. *Roll each piece into a strand 10 cm (4 in) long.*

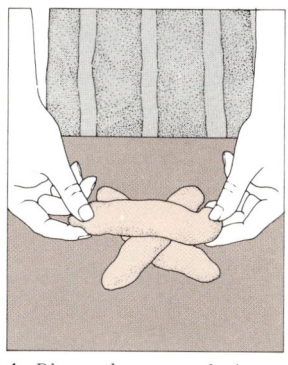

4. *Place the strands into a star shape with the centers crossing on top of each other.*

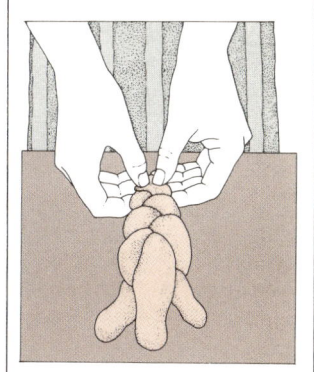

5. *Plait the bottom three strands as you would for a three strand plait.*

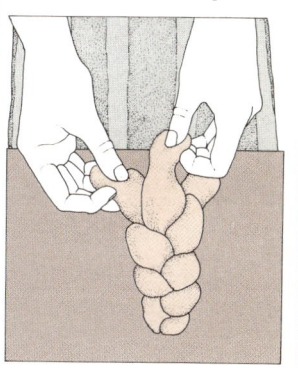

6. *Then turn the piece around and plait the other three strands.*

Twists - continued

TWISTS AND PLAITS

7. Place on a pre-greased baking sheet. Eggwash and sprinkle lightly down the center with poppy seeds.

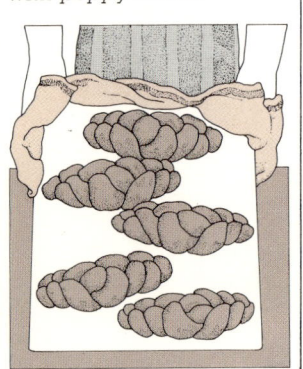

8. Let rise and bake at 220°C (425°F) for 15 to 20 minutes.

How to make a coil

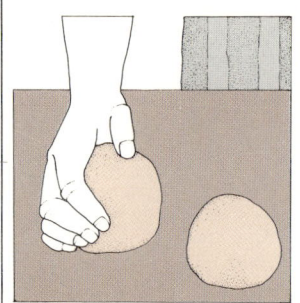

1. Take an 85g (6 Tbs) dough piece and mould into a ball. Rest for 5 minutes.

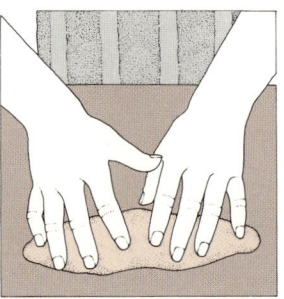

2. Roll the dough into a strand 23cm (9in) long.

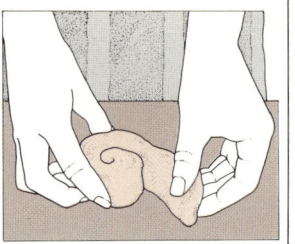

3. Hold one end of the strand between the thumb and forefinger of one hand, and with the other hand take the other end of the dough strand bringing it around the first end in a coil.

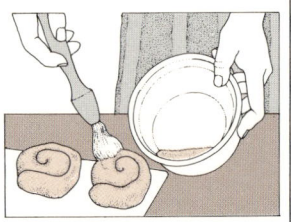

4. Place on a pre-greased baking sheet and eggwash. Prove and bake at 220°C (425°F) for 15 to 20 minutes.

FRUIT BREADS

1. Basic dough
2. Yorkshire tea cakes
3. Fruit plaits
4. Sticky buns
5. Lattice tea bread
6. Cinnamon slice
7. Apple köcken
8. Stollen
9. Chelsea tea ring
10. Bara – brith
11. Fruit malt bread
12. Walnut fruit loaf

Fruit breads and rich tea cakes

Many of the most popular tea-time breads and cakes are made with a simple, sweetened, bread dough – sometimes containing dried fruit, sometimes not.

This section contains recipes for a dozen of these breads – all deriving from the one basic dough but producing a considerable variety of end product.

Fruit & tea breads—Basic recipe

Ingredients:

450g	flour	4 cups
85g	oil or unsalted fat	6 Tbs
85g	sugar	6 Tbs
7g	salt	1 Tsp
85g	yeast	6 Tbs
	milk	7/8 cups
	1 large egg	

For fruit dough add currants or white raisins

This recipe can be used as the basis for many a varied type of fruit or tea bread. The addition of dried fruit to a dough is an effective way of sweetening the bread – as well as adding new and interesting flavors – because the fruit contains its own sugar. If the fruit is warmed before it is added to the dough it will be easier to distribute evenly.

Rub the fat and salt into the flour. Pre-boil the milk and allow to cool to lukewarm temperature (approx 32°C/90°F). Stir in the sugar until dissolved, crumble in the yeast and whisk until that has also dissolved. (If Method II is used, keep 115g (8 Tbs) of the flour to make the ferment.)

Add the liquid to the flour mixture and mix to a dough. Knead well until a soft silky dough is achieved.

This type of dough is usually stickier than the normal bread doughs because of the high sugar concentration in the recipe, so do not try to stiffen it up by adding a lot more flour.

Rest the dough for 15 minutes before punching down, and then rest for a further 15 minutes.

The fruit (if desired) may now be added and moulded into the dough.

The dough is then ready for moulding into one of many alternative shapes, but the best shape for nearly all fruit *loaves* is the traditional bread tin – so you can make your fruit bread without any extra equipment. Fruit loaves should be glazed, just before the end of baking, with a syrup made from milk and sugar.

Yorkshire tea cakes 2

Measure the dough into twelve 85g (6 Tbs) pieces and mould each piece into a ball. Cover with a cloth and leave for 15 minutes to recover.

With a rolling pin, roll out each piece into a circular shape about 11cm (4½in) in diameter and place them on a baking sheet about 13mm (½in) apart and leave to rise until ready. (See 'rising' if you are in doubt as to when they are ready.)

Bake in a fairly hot oven 220°C (425°F) for 10 to 15 minutes or until golden brown in color. Allow to cool on racks.

Fruit plaits 3

Divide the dough into three 340g (¾ cup) pieces. Further divide each piece into three equal parts (115g/¼ cup).

Roll each piece under your hand into a baton-shaped strand about 23-25cm (9-10in) long.

Arrange the three strands into a fan shape with the narrow closed ends placed on top of each other and a weight put on the top to hold these ends together. Take the dough piece on the left and lift it over the center piece at the same time pulling the center strand out to the left. Repeat the process using the right strand, and so on until the end of the plait, and then pinch the ends together.

Place the plaits on a baking sheet and let rise for about 20 minutes or until ready.

Bake in a moderately hot oven at 205°C (400°F), for about 15 to 20 minutes.

When baked, place on a rack to cool. When cool, spread with thin sugar icing and sprinkle the top liberally with chopped glacé cherries and flaked almonds or chopped nuts.

NB The plaiting of this bread follows the same method as that described in the section on plaiting (*see page 64*).

FRUIT BREAD

Sticky buns 4

Roll the whole dough piece out into an oblong shape approximately 30cm × 38cm (12in × 15in) and brush the whole piece with melted butter or margarine.

Sprinkle 115g (¼ cup) currants over the whole piece apart from a 2.5cm (1in) strip along the bottom edge of the dough. Then roll the dough from the top to the bottom rather like a Swiss roll.

When the roll is complete cut into slices about 2.5cm (1in) thick and lay each piece into a 2.5cm (1in) deep square baking tin. Allow the dough pieces to touch and fill the whole tin.

Allow to rise for 20 to 30 minutes and then sprinkle with sugar.

Bake for 15 to 20 minutes in a moderate oven at 205°C (400°F).

Lattice tea bread 5

Take a 340g (¾ cup) piece of dough and roll into a 6mm (¼in) thick oblong 30cm × 20cm (12in × 8in). Down each long side make 5cm (2in) deep angled cuts 13mm (½in) apart.

Spread the center with apricot jam and the sprinkle thickly with currants, raisins and chopped cherries.

Bring the cut strips, first left and then right, into the center so that they overlap. Continue until you reach the bottom.

Wash the whole piece with egg and let rise for 15 to 20 minutes.

Bake at 205°C (400°F). When baked, allow to cool and then dredge with sugar icing.

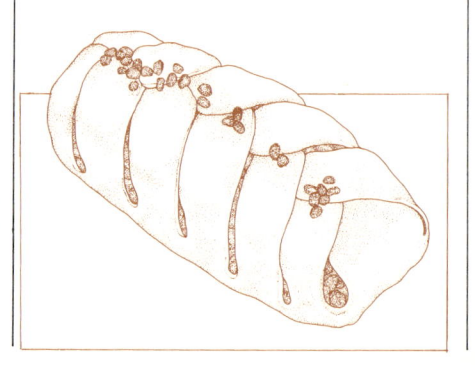

Cinnamon slice

Roll the whole dough into a square 38cm × 38cm (15in × 15in). Spread a thin layer of apricot jam 13cm (5in) across the center of the square.

Mix 85g (¼ cup) sugar with 30g (2 Tbs) cinnamon and sprinkle half of the mixture over the jam. Then fold the top third of the dough over the middle piece with the jam and cinnamon mix on it. Spread the rest of the cinnamon/sugar mixture on top of the fold allowing a 13mm (½in) strip of dough clear at the top. Bring the bottom third of the dough over the folds and seal it well down along the edge. Wash the top of the dough with egg and with a knife mark out 4cm (1½in) slices across the piece.

Let rise on a baking tray for 20 to 30 minutes and then bake in a moderate oven at 205°C (400°F).

When baked, allow to cool on a rack and then spread with a thin layer of sugar icing.

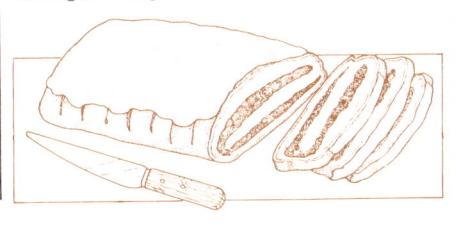

Apple köcken

Additional Ingredients:

115g (½ cup) apples (lightly stewed)
sugar to taste

Measure a 225g (6 cups) piece of dough. Mould it round into a ball and leave under a cloth to recover for 10 minutes.

Pin the dough piece out to form a circle of about 25cm (10in) diameter. In the bottom half of the dough circle spread 115g (¼ cup) of lightly stewed or tinned apples, sprinkled with sugar. Allow at least 2.5cm (1in) of plain dough round the edge, and slightly dampen the edge of the bottom half of the circle with water. Fold the top part of the circle down over the apples so that the edges meet and press them well together with the fingertips. Make a small hole in the top of the dough with a knife or scissors. Place on a baking sheet and let rise for 20 to 30 minutes.

Bake at 205°C (400°F) for 15 to 20 minutes. Cool on a wire.

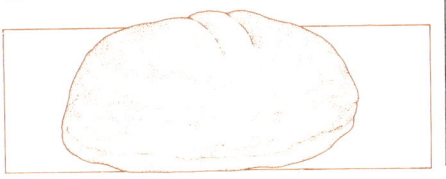

FRUIT BREAD

Stollen

Additional Ingredients:

85g	glacé cherries	6 Tbs
170g	almond paste	12 Tbs

Take a 450g (4 cups) dough piece and mould it into a ball and cover with a cloth. Leave to rest for 10 minutes.

Roll the dough out into a 30cm (12in) circle and wash with egg or water.

Leaving a clear 13mm ($\frac{1}{2}$in) edge, spread the whole of the bottom half of the circle with chopped glacé cherries (saving a few for decoration). With the hands, mould the almond paste or marzipan into a 25cm (10in) roll and place it on top of the cherries just below the center of the circle, again ensuring that the edges are clear.

Fold the top half of the dough down over the bottom until the edges meet and press them well together.

Eggwash the top of the stollen and put on a baking sheet to rise for 30 minutes.

Bake at 190°C (375°F) for 20 to 25 minutes.

Allow to cool on a rack and then cover with a layer of sugar icing. Before the icing sets, sprinkle liberally with the rest of the chopped cherries and a few chopped nuts.

Chelsea tea ring

Take a 225g (2 cups) dough piece and mould it into a ball. Cover with a cloth and leave to recover for 10 minutes.

Pin out into an 18cm (7in) circle and wash the surface with egg. With the flat of the hand pick the dough piece up from underneath and drop it (egg side down) onto a dish of sugar. Take the dough out of the sugar and place it on a baking sheet.

Across the sugared top of the dough mark well with a knife into six slices (as though you were cutting a cake).

Put half a glacé cherry on each of these slices 2cm ($\frac{3}{4}$in) in from the edge with a whole cherry in the center.

Let rise for 30 minutes and bake at 205°C (400°F) for 10 to 15 minutes.

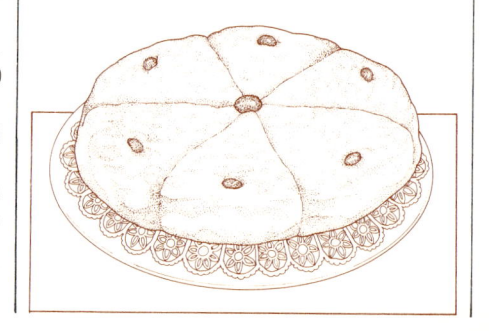

Fruit malt bread

Ingredients		
450g	flour	4 cups
60g	malt flour *dark*	½ cup
45g	malt extract	3 Tbs
15g	salt	1 Tbs
30g	unsalted butter or oil	2 Tbs
30g	molasses	2 Tbs
45g	soft brown sugar	⅓ cups
30g	yeast	2 Tbs
	pinch of baking powder	
340ml	water *lukewarm*	1½ cups
250g	raisins	1 cup

Sift together the flour, malt flour, salt and baking powder. Rub the fat well in and make a well.

Dissolve the malt extract, molasses and sugar into the water, crumble in the yeast and stir well.

Pour the liquor into the well and draw in the flour until a soft sticky dough is obtained. Cover with a cloth and leave in a warm draft-free place for 2 to 2½ hours.

Add the raisins and mould them into the dough until they are evenly distributed. Weigh the dough into three 420g (15oz) pieces and gently mould into loaf shapes.

Place each piece onto a baking sheet and cover with an inverted (4 cups) loaf tin.

Leave to rise for a further 1–1½ hours. Bake in a 350°F oven for 1 hour.

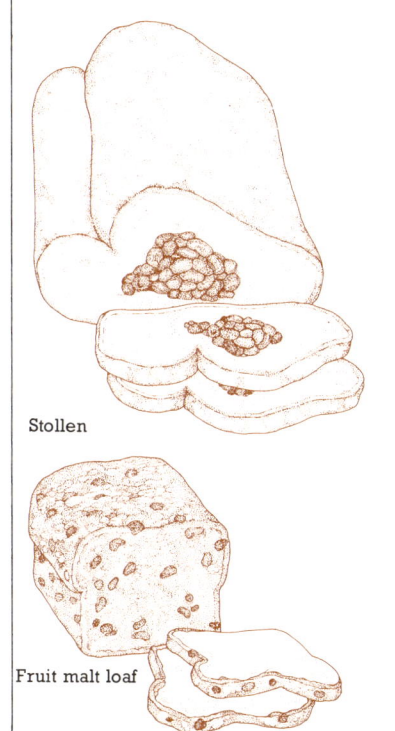

Stollen

Fruit malt loaf

Walnut fruit loaf

Ingredients

450g	flour	4 cups
30g	unsalted butter or oil	2 Tbs
30g	sugar	2 Tbs
	pinch of salt	
30g	yeast	2 Tbs
0.3 litre	milk *lukewarm*	1 cup
225g	fruit *(currants, light or dark raisins or a mixture)*	1 cup
90g	walnuts	6 Tbs

Sift salt and flour together. Rub in the fat and make a well. Dissolve the sugar into the milk, crumble in the yeast and mix well. Pour the liquor into the well and draw in the flour to form a dough.

Knead the dough well until it is smooth and silky.

Cover with a cloth and leave in a warm draft-free place for 30 minutes.

Punch down the dough at the same time incorporating the fruit and nuts. Rest for a further 30 minutes.

Two loaves can be made from this recipe or, if preferred, plaits of small buns may also be produced to give a variety.

Bake in a moderately hot oven 420°F–440°F. The loaves should take 35 to 40 minutes. Smaller loaves or buns take less time depending on their size.

The addition of nuts to this dough will increase the fat content and further enrich the loaf. If you like a particularly rich fruit loaf you can experiment with the addition of other fruits. Dates, for example, are especially good with walnuts. Dried apricots and prunes are also worth considering (they need to be well chopped before mixing in) but, for a rich, well-balanced fruit loaf, a combination of raisins, dates and walnuts would be very hard to better.

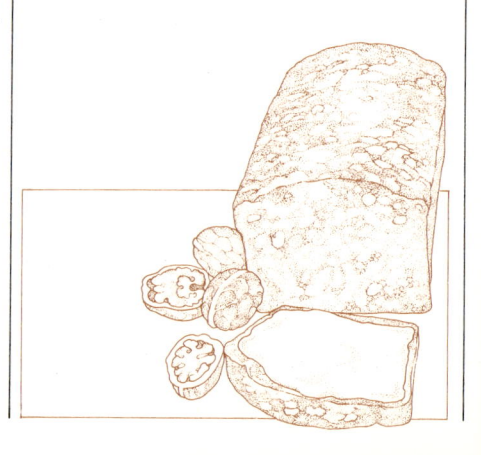

Bara-Brith (Welsh fruit loaf)

Ingredients:

450g	flour	4 cups
85g	unsalted butter	6 Tbs
85g	sugar	6 Tbs
7g	salt	1 Tsp
115g	yeast	8 Tbs
85ml	water *lukewarm*	⅓ cup
85g	currants	6 Tbs
85g	sultanas	6 Tbs
30g	mixed peel	2 Tbs
¼ teaspoon	cinnamon	
¼ teaspoon	nutmeg	
¼ teaspoon	mixed spice	

Sift the flour and spices together. Rub the salt and the fat well into the flour and make a well. Pour the eggs into the well.

Put the sugar into the water and stir until dissolved. Crumble in the yeast and again stir until dissolved.

Pour the yeast mixture into the well with the eggs and draw in the flour until you have a soft sticky dough. Knead the dough until it is clear (all flour and liquid evenly mixed throughout), this should take about 3 to 4 minutes. Add the fruit to the dough and knead carefully until it is evenly distributed.

Place the dough into a floured bowl and cover with a cloth. Leave until the bulk has doubled in volume (this can take from 1 to 2 hours), punching down once in that time. When the dough is ready punch it down once more and then split into two equal pieces.

Mould into loaf shapes and put them into well greased small loaf tins.

Allow to rise, until the dough is 13mm (½in) above the top of the tin. This will take 40 to 60 minutes, so make sure that the rising atmosphere is correct otherwise a thick skin will form and inhibit the volume of the loaf.

When risen bake at 180°C (350°F), for 50 to 60 minutes.

When ready, take the loaves out of the tins and allow to cool on racks.

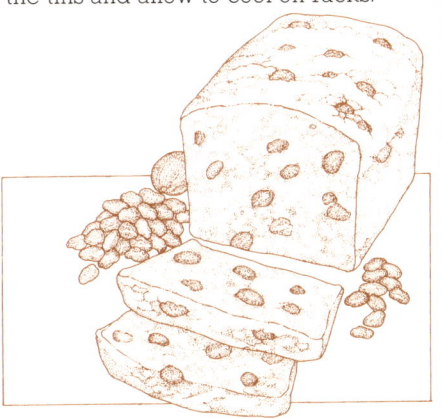

INTERNATIONAL

1 French bread
2 Rye bread
3 Sweet and sour bread
4 Wholewheat pizza base
5 Bagels
6 Beer bread
7 Hot cross buns

International recipes

Although many of the recipes in the rest of this book have international variations, this section concentrates on breads which have special significance either internationally, or in their countries of origin.

French bread 1

Ingredients:

280g	flour	2 cups
15g	yeast	1 Tbs
¼ litre	water	1 cup
½ teaspoon	sugar	
170g	flour	1⅔ cups

(to add after ferment has been made)

The long crispy French stick is now very popular, not only in France, but all over Europe and America. With cheese or cooked meats and pickles there is nothing nicer than fresh French bread. To make it successfully, steam is essential in the baking process. This recipe, therefore, is definitely not suitable for use in an electric oven where the heating elements are exposed. Usually, a French stick would be 500–600mm (20–24in) in length. For home baking, however, it would be more practical to halve this length.

Method:

Dissolve the sugar and yeast in the water and stir well in. Add the flour and, using the fingers, roughly disperse it in the water until you have a lumpy stiff ferment. Cover with a cloth and set aside in a draft-free place for one hour, or until the volume has roughly doubled.

Dissolve a further 15g (1 Tbs) salt in 60ml (¼ cup) hand warm water and pour into the ferment, mixing lightly for a few seconds. The ferment will drop, so add the remaining 170g (⅔ cup) flour and make it into a dough.

When the dough is mixed, turn it onto the working surface and start to knead, adding extra flour if necessary. Kneading should be continued for only two or three minutes with this dough. Cover with a cloth and set aside in a cool draft-free place for 30 minutes.

Set the oven to 230°C (450°F), and place a clean loaf pan in the top of the oven. Immediately prior to baking, the pan should be moved to the bottom, or 'sole', of the oven.

When bulk fermentation is complete, divide the dough into three pieces and mould into balls. Let them rest for five minutes before rolling the dough pieces out by hand into batons about 250mm (10in) long.

With a sharp knife make six or seven diagonal cuts across each stick. Spread a clean cloth on your working surface and sprinkle it with flour. Place the dough pieces onto the cloth, making sure that they are kept straight, and cover them with a second cloth. Leave to rise for 20–30 minutes. When the sticks are risen, transfer them to a baking tin, taking great care not to punch them down.

Place the bread in the top of the oven (remember the hot loaf pan should now be at the bottom) and pour ¾ cup of water into the loaf pan. Close the door immediately, allowing the steam from the hot pan to fill the oven. After 10 minutes reduce the oven heat to 205°C (400°F) and open the oven door for 30 seconds to allow the steam to clear and to remove the loaf pan. Bake for a further 7–10 minutes until the sticks are a rich golden brown all over and do not bend when picked up at one end. Remove from the oven and cool on wires.

French sticks do not keep very long and should be eaten very fresh for maximum enjoyment. If you are not going to use them on the same day you can freshen them by dampening them slightly with a clean wet cloth and then putting them in a hot oven for five minutes.

Rye bread

Ingredients:

450g	rye meal	4 cups
450g	flour white or graham	4 cups
30g	salt	2 Tbs
30g	sugar	2 Tbs
30g	fat or oil	2 Tbs
0.6 litre	water *lukewarm*	1 cup
30g	yeast	2 Tbs

Dissolve the sugar into the water. Crumble in the yeast and whisk until lump free.

To the liquid, add 225g (2 cups) of the white or brown flour (not the rye meal) and stir until smooth. Set aside for 15 to 20 minutes until the ferment is ready.

Rub the rest of the flour, rye meal, fat and salt together and make a well.

When the ferment is ready pour it into the flour well. Draw in the flour until a dough is formed and knead for 10 to 15 minutes.

Cover with a cloth and leave for 1 to 1½ hours punching down once during this time.

After bulk fermentation is complete punch down the dough well and rest for 2 minutes.

Ball the dough up into two equal pieces and place them onto a pre-greased baking sheet. Flatten the dough a little with the palm of the hand. Eggwash the dough pieces and set aside.

Let rise for 30 to 40 minutes and bake at 230°C (450°F) for 40 minutes.

Rye bread is still much used in Eastern Europe and in Jewish communities, but has fallen into disuse elsewhere. This is a pity, because the strong flavor of the bread is quite different to that made from wheat flours. Rye meals can be bought in dark or light varieties and can be used in sweet bread and yeast cakes.

Sweet & sour bread 3

Ingredients:

450g	rye flour	4 cups
340g	white flour	3 cups
30g	salt	2 Tbs
30g	sugar	2 Tbs
½ litre	water *lukewarm*	2 cups
60g	oil	4 Tbs
30g	yeast	2 Tbs
20g	caraway seeds	1½ Tbs

This type of bread is much favored by the Jewish community and has a most unusual and interesting flavor.

Ideally, the bread should be made with a 'sour' dough. This is an old dough which has been kept unbaked for some time. If you are intending to make rye bread, make a little extra dough and keep it in a covered container in the pantry until you wish to make some more rye bread or this sweet and sour loaf. Then just add it to the normal recipe at the final stage of mixing the dough. This bread can be made, however, without a sour dough and produces very good results.

In the U.S., sourdough has many sophisticated variations and can be made with rye, white or wholewheat flours.

Dissolve the sugar into the water, crumble in the yeast and stir. Add the white flour and mix until smooth and lump free. Set aside for 30 minutes.

Rub the oil and salt into the rye flour and make a well. When the ferment is ready pour it into the well and draw up. If you do have any sour dough now is the time to add it.

Knead the dough well for 10 to 15 minutes. Cover and leave for 1 hour or until the bulk has doubled in volume. Punch down once after 30 minutes.

After bulk fermentation is complete punch down the dough, and at the same time incorporate the caraway seeds into the dough. Mix until the seeds are evenly distributed.

Rest the dough for 2 minutes. Cut into two equal pieces and mould into ball shapes.

Place the pieces on to pre-greased sheet tins.

Flatten the tops slightly with the palm of the hand, eggwash and sprinkle caraway seeds on top of the loaves.

Let rise for 40 to 50 minutes and bake in a hot oven at 230°C (450°F) for 40 minutes. Cool the bread on racks in the usual way.

Beer bread

Ingredients:

250g	wholewheat flour	2¼ cups
250g	white flour	2¼ cups
0.3 litre	beer or stout	1 cup
30g	yeast	2 Tbs
60g	soft brown sugar	4 Tbs
15g	salt	1 Tbs
	large egg	
60g	fat or oil	4 Tbs

It has been said that this bread never fails. This seems to be rather an extravagant claim, but it is a remarkably easy recipe and one that requires no unusual skills. Perhaps the success of this bread, which is said to have originated in Belgium, is due to the fact that beer, unless it is completely flat, contains some unfermented sugar and some still active yeast cells. The affinity between brewer's yeast and the variety used by bakers is probably sufficient to ensure a high level of yeast activity and, therefore, a lot of carbon dioxide.

Method:

Mix the flour, salt and fat to a fine crumbly consistency and make a well. Break the egg into the well. Dissolve the sugar in the beer, crumble in the yeast and mix until evenly dispersed. Pour the beer and yeast mixture into the well and make up the dough. Knead for 10 minutes. Cover with a damp cloth and set in a warm draft-free place for 40 minutes, punching down once halfway through the ferment.

After bulk fermentation has been completed, knead and mould the dough into a loaf shape and then put it into a well greased 900g (2lb) loaf tin. Prove in a warm humid atmosphere until the dough has approximately doubled in size. Bake in a fairly hot oven, 205°C (400°F), for 45–50 minutes. Cool on racks – and cheers!

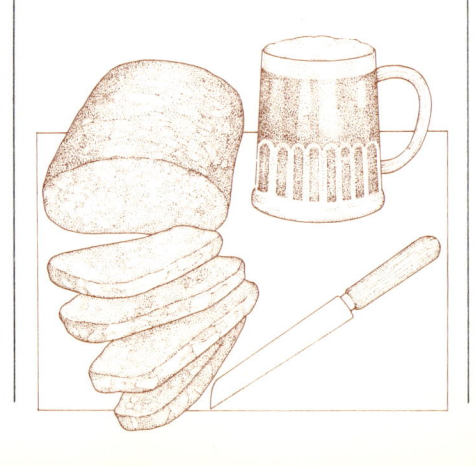

Pizza base (Wholewheat)

Ingredients:

225g	wholewheat flour	2 cups
115g	graham flour	1 cup
30g	oil or fat	¼ cup
30g	sugar	2 Tbs
7g	salt	1 Tsp
170ml	water *lukewarm*	¾ cup
15g	yeast	1 Tbs

This recipe gives a deliciously different pizza, making the dish not only more tasty but also more nutritious.

The wholewheat pizza base is ideal for freezing and if you wish to do so you can make a whole batch of bases at one time. For freezing, roll the pieces out to size and place between two sheets of greaseproof or wax paper and freeze immediately. When you wish to use the dough bases remove them from the freezer an hour before baking and add the pizza topping.

Method:

Rub the oil and salt into the wholewheat and brown flours. Make a well.

Dissolve the sugar in the water, crumble in the yeast and stir into the water.

Pour the liquid into the well and draw in the flour to make a dough.

Knead for 8 to 10 minutes. Make the dough into a ball and let it rest for 10 minutes.

Roll the dough out so that it will cover a 25cm (10in) oven proof plate.

Cover the dough with your favorite pizza topping and let it rest for 15 minutes.

Bake at 205°C (400°F), for 20 minutes or until the pizza topping is cooked. Serve immediately.

Wholewheat flour can be used for many recipes other than bread, but pizza dough is one for which it is better than other flours.

Hot cross buns

Ingredients:

Dough:

450g	flour	4 cups
30g	unsalted butter	2 Tbs
15g	salt	1 Tbs
	large egg	
¼ teaspoon	nutmeg	
¼ teaspoon	cinnamon	
¼ teaspoon	mixed spice	
60g	raisins	4 Tbs
60g	currants	4 Tbs
30g	mixed peel	2 Tbs

Ferment:

0.3 litre	milk *warm*	1 cup
30g	yeast	2 Tbs
90g	sugar	6 Tbs

Cross paste:

60g	flour	4 Tbs
30ml	water	⅛ cup
30ml	oil	⅛ cup
	pinch salt	

The origins of hot cross buns

Spiced buns have been known in England since the early 16th Century, and were originally baked only for special and festive occasions – Good Friday being one of them. It was natural, therefore, for the Good Friday bun to become the hot cross bun which is now the symbol of the English Easter.

Ferment method:

Pour the warm milk into a mixing bowl and stir in the sugar, yeast and flour until a light, lump free batter is achieved. Set the bowl aside in a warm draft free place until the ferment has doubled in volume – about 20 minutes.

Dough method:

Add the salt to the flour and rub in the fat until the mixture is of a light crumbly texture. Make a well in the center. Break the egg into the well and when the ferment is ready pour that in with the egg. Carefully draw the flour into the ferment until you have a soft dough. If the dough is still stiff at this stage, add a little more warm milk.

Knead the dough well for about 10 minutes until it is clear. Cover with a cloth and leave in a warm draft-free place for 30 minutes. Punch down well and replace the cloth for another 30 minutes.

After the bulk fermentation is complete add the currants, raisins and mixed peel and mould carefully into the dough until they are well dispersed. Rest the mixture for a further 10 minutes.

Measure the dough into 90g (⅞ cup)

pieces and mould round. Place them on lightly greased baking tins, pressing each one out a little, and let rise in the usual way.

Cross paste

While the buns are rising, you can make the cross paste. Mix the water, oil, salt and flour together until smooth and runny, then pour the mixture into a greaseproof piping bag.

When the buns have risen, carefully pipe a cross on the top of each and put them into a pre-heated oven at 205°C (400°F) for 15–20 minutes.

While the buns are baking, boil 60g (4 Tbs) sugar in 30ml (½ cup) water until dissolved, then simmer for 5–10 minutes. When the buns are baked, put them onto a cooling rack and brush them with the sugar glaze.

THE GOOD FRIDAY BUN

When the cross first appeared on these buns is uncertain, but they were common in the mid 19th Century and it is likely, in view of what the Victorians did to Christmas, that they were responsible for the cross on the bun. Certainly, there are many references to hot cross buns in the 1840's and 1850's, but there will probably never be any certainty about their first appearance.

Hot Cross Buns

Bagels

Ingredients:

675g	strong white flour	6 cups
30g	yeast	2 Tbs
15g	salt	1 Tbs
30g	corn oil	2 Tbs
0.4 litre	water *lukewarm*	1⅔ cups

Bagels are very popular Jewish breakfast buns. They are delicious hot with bacon and eggs and can turn an ordinary breakfast into a feast. The making of bagels differs from that of ordinary bread in that they are not left to rise in the usual way, but dropped into boiling water for a few seconds before baking. This process brings the starch in the flour to the surface of the bun and, when baked, gives a very high gloss and crisp surface to the finished bagel.

Method:

Dissolve the yeast into ¼ litre (1 cup) of the water. When it is clear, add 225g (2 cups) of the flour and mix to make a rough ferment. Set the bowl aside in a warm draft-free place and cover with a damp cloth. Leave the ferment to double in volume – this will take 30–40 minutes.

When the ferment is ready, dissolve the salt in the remaining 140ml (⅔ cup) of the water and pour into the ferment. Mix the liquid lightly and then add the rest of the flour. Mix into a stiff dough and incorporate the oil, kneading all the time until the dough, although stiff, is smooth and clear. Cover the dough with a cloth and let it rest for one hour, punching down once during that period.

When bulk fermentation has been completed, knead the dough well for two minutes and then cut it into 115g (1 cup) pieces and mould each piece into a ball. Allow the dough pieces to rest for a further five minutes.

Roll each dough ball into a strand about 200mm (8in) in length, take a strand of dough and wrap it once round three or four fingers of your hand, allowing the ends to overlap by about 2.5cm (1in). Roll the overlapping ends together on the working surface until a uniform thickness is achieved and the dough piece forms a circle. Set the dough circles to rest for 15 minutes.

Put a large pan of water on the stove to boil and when the dough pieces are ready drop them, three or four at a time, into the boiling water and leave them until they float to the surface. Use a wire scoop to remove the bagels from the water and place them immediately onto lightly greased baking tins. Put them into a hot oven, 230°C (450°F). Do not wait for all the bagels to boil before starting to bake; place them on sheets and bake them as soon as they are ready.

When they have been baking for 10 minutes, use a spatula to turn them over on the sheets and continue baking until they are golden brown.

BAGEL VARIATIONS

Bagels lend themselves ideally to a number of savoury fillings, the best known being smoked salmon and cream cheese – a great favorite in New York. Other meats and smoked fish are almost as good, and probably less expensive. For other interesting flavors try the suggestions below.

'Lox' and bagel
Bagels filled with smoked salmon and cream cheese.

Caraway bagels
Brush the tops of fresh bagels with melted butter and scatter caraway seeds over the top.

Onion bagels
Brush the top of the bagels with a mixture of chopped cooked onion and butter.

Fault finding

Measuring the ingredients

There are no secrets or mysteries about making good bread, but it is not achieved by slavish adherence to recipes. Things will go wrong, especially in the early stages, and nobody makes perfect bread all the time. By trial-and-error you will discover what affects your bread adversely, and also what produces good results. You will gradually build up your own pattern of breadmaking and will be able to keep faults to a minimum.

Most faults and the usual causes of them can be found in the chart overleaf. As you will see, there are a number of possible causes for each fault and this may appear to be rather daunting. You will find, however, through a process of elimination, that you can easily narrow it down to one or two 'suspects'. One of the chief causes of trouble is the measuring of ingredients, especially when making a quantity of dough that differs from the method or recipe that you are using. Some ingredients, particularly yeast, should not be increased or decreased in strict proportion to the amount of flour used. For example, ½oz (15g) of yeast is usually sufficient for 1lb (450g) of flour, but when using 3lb (1.35kg) of flour it is rarely necessary to use more than 1oz (30g) of yeast. To use more might result in the bread tasting yeasty.

Liquids

Getting the amount of water right is something which can only be learned by practice. Different flours will absorb different amounts of water, so remember that quantities given in recipes are only a guide. Water affects nearly every characteristic of the loaf: volume, texture, shape and crust. The temperature, too, is important – overheat the water and you may kill the yeast. Milk is an important liquid in breadmaking. Its chief effects, as we have seen, are to enrich the loaf and soften the crust but, if too much is used, the texture and shape of the loaf may suffer.

Fat

Fat, both the amount and the type, has a striking effect upon dough. Many bakers say that, of all fats, only butter gives a good result. Others may say that it is better to make bread without fat. The latter view is understandable if the loaf in question is a simple, basic bread. Some recipes, however, notably brioche and croissant, could not be

Fault finding

made without fat. The problem with fats is that they are probably more unstable and subject to change than the other ingredients of bread. Butter, particularly, deteriorates fairly rapidly and it is important that fat used in breadmaking should be fresh. It is hard to generalize, but one can say that most faults that are due to fats result through using too much.

Salt

Like water, the behavior of salt in bread dough is fundamental. It will make a very considerable difference to the flavor of the loaf if used in too large or small amounts, and it can have a dramatic effect upon every other aspect. Quite apart from anything else, the moisture retaining qualities of salt are vital to bread, but a loaf made without it will not only dry out and become stale quickly, it will also be flavorless.

The amount of salt you choose to put into your bread will, ultimately, depend upon your palate, but it is worth noting here that the recipes given in this book recommend an amount which is unlikely to be too high. You may well find that you can satisfactorily increase the quantity.

The only other thing that can usefully be said here is that one baker's fault may be another's ideal. This hardly applies to bread which is utterly tasteless or which falls apart when cut, but there are plenty of people who like their bread to have a texture which is open to the point of being 'holed', or which has a hard crust. Perhaps the loaf that is devoid of any 'faults' is nobody's favorite, but that is irrelevant. The purpose of this book is to help you make the bread you want to make, and the purpose of this section is to help you identify the cause of anything you find unsatisfactory.

Faults

As you can see from the chart on this page, there are many common faults in breadmaking. There are, unfortunately, many possible causes for each fault. Only by a process of trial and error can you be sure of identifying exactly what has gone wrong. Hopefully, you will not need to refer to the chart too frequently.

FAULT	POSSIBLE CAUSES
SMALL VOLUME	Flour too soft; too little yeast; too much salt; too much, or too little, water; too much sugar; dough allowed to become too hot or too cold; fermentation too long or to short; insufficient final rising; oven too hot
HIGH VOLUME	Too much yeast; too little salt; final rising too long; oven too cool
POOR CRUST COLOR	Too little salt; dough too hot; fermentation too long; skin formed on dough; oven too cool
HIGH CRUST COLOR	Too much salt; too much milk; too much sugar; fermentation too short; oven too hot
CRUST CRACK	Too little water; too much milk; insufficient final rising
BAD SHAPE	Flour too soft; too little salt; too little, or too much, water; too much milk; too much sugar; fermentation too long; poor moulding; scumming; oven too hot
COARSE TEXTURE	Flour too soft; too much water; final rising too long; poor moulding; oven too hot or too cool
CRUMBLY TEXTURE	Too much yeast; too little salt; too little water; too much fat; dough too hot; fermentation too long, or too short; final rising too long
STREAKS AND CORES	Too much fat; dough too hot or too cold; scumming
HOLES	Too little yeast; too much salt; too little water; too much fat; dough too hot or too cold; fermentation too long or too short; final rising too long or too short; pour moulding; oven too hot or too cool
POOR CRUMB COLOR	Flour too soft; too much yeast; too little salt; too much or too little water; dough too hot; fermentation too long; final rising too long; scumming; oven too cool

CONVERSION CHART

Table of conversion for solids and liquids; the metric equivalents have been slightly adjusted to suit the recipes in this book.

Ounces	pounds (lb) – pints	grams	millilitres (ml) centilitres (cl)
¼		7	7ml
½		15	15ml
1		30	30ml
2		60	60ml
3		90	90ml
3½		100	100ml
4	¼lb	120	120ml
5		150	150ml
6		180	180ml
7		210	210ml
8	½lb	225	225ml
9		250	¼ litre
10	½ pint	285	28.5cl
12	¾lb	340	34cl
14		400	40cl
15	¾ pint	425	42.5cl
16	1lb	450	45cl
18		500	½ litre
20	1 pint	560	56cl
24	1½ lb	680	68cl
25		710	71cl
27		770	77cl
28		800	80cl
30	1½ pints	850	85cl
32	2lb	900	90cl
36		1kg	1 litre
40	2 pints (1 quart)	1.12kg	112cl

Glossary of terms

Aleurone
The innermost skin of the wheat grain, Aleurone is part of what we call bran – and the most nutritious part. It contains essential vitamins and minerals.

Ascorbic Acid
The form of vitamin C which can be used in certain breads to speed up the aerating or leavening process.

Bran
The hard outer 'shell' of the wheat grain. It consists of five layers, or skins, and is the part discarded in the milling of white flour.

Bulk Fermentation
The dough recovery period in between mixing the dough and moulding it into shape.

Clear Dough
Fully kneaded dough which has no flour, water or fat streaks in it.

Endosperm
The starchy inner part of the wheat grain – flour is chiefly composed of the endosperm.

Extraction
In the milling process, it is usual to discard some, or all, of the bran. Confusingly, the *extraction rate* of a particular flour refers to the amount which is left, not the amount removed. For example, a flour of 85% extraction has had 15% (consisting of bran) extracted. White flour, from which all (or almost all) of the bran has been removed, is usually about 73%. Genuine wholewheat flour should be described on the wrapper as 100%.

Fermentation
Process of the yeast working with flour, sugar and water, producing carbon dioxide and alcohol.

Flying Top
When the top crust of the loaf has cracked away from the rest of the loaf – usually due to under rising.

Germ
The part of the grain which contains the embryo root and growing shoots of the new plant. Especially valuable as a source of vitamin E.

Gluten
An elastic substance produced by the

protein in wheat. Because of its elasticity it can hold the gasses produced by the action of yeast and expand with them – thus causing the loaf to rise.

Green Dough
Dough which is taken and moulded before it has had sufficient time to develop in bulk fermentation.

Moulding
Shaping the dough.

Oven Flash
Too hot an oven causing excessive color to the bread crust, without the bread being properly baked.

Oven Spring
The increased volume of the bread caused by the initial oven heat before the yeast is killed and the loaf has set.

Punching Down
Re-kneading the dough to expel carbon dioxide and incorporate oxygen – also having the effect of reducing the bulk of the dough.

Resting or Intermediate Proof
Resting the completed dough immediately prior to final moulding. This, almost literally, means giving the dough the chance to get its breath back.

Rising
Period of time between final moulding of the dough and the start of the baking.

Roll
Roll out with a rolling pin.

Scum
Crusting of the raw dough due to drafts or insufficient moisture in the atmosphere.

Sour Dough
Old dough which can be used as a fermentation aid in breadmaking.

Sponge
Mixture of yeast, water, flour and sugar used in the ferment and dough methods.

Well
An area cleared in the center of prepared flour to make a receptacle for the liquid.

Index

Figures in italics refer to illustrations

Additives, 20
Almond paste, 74
America, 18, 22, 86–7
Anti-depressant, 6
Apple köcken, *30–1*, 73
Apricots, 29, 76
Ascorbic acid, 24
Austria, 26

Bagels, *30–1*, 86–7
Bara-Brith, *30–1*, 77
Barley, 12
Basic recipes, 32–3, 40–4
Beer bread, *30–1*, 82
Bloomer loaf, *30–1*, 47
Bran, 13, 21
Brioches, *30–1*, 56–9
Brown bread, 9, 20–3, *30–1*, 50–1
Brown flours, 20–1
Buckwheat, 12
Bulk fermentation, 24–5, 28, 34, 36

Calcium, 20
Canada, 7, 18, 22
Canary Islands, 27
Caraway seeds, 29, 81
Caraway bagel, 87
Carbohydrates, 6, 20
Chelsea tea ring, *30–1*, 74
Cherries, glacé, 71–2, 74
Chocolate rolls, 55
Christmas loaves, 26
Cinnamon, 29, 77, 84
Cinnamon slice, *30–1*, 73
Cob loaf, *30–1*, 48
Coburg loaf, *30–1*, 48
Coil loaf, *30–1*, 63, 68

Commercial baking, *10–11*
Constituents of bread, 6, 20
Cooling, 41
Corkscrew loaf, *30–1*, 63, 66
Corn, 12
Cottage loaf, *30–1*, 37, 47
Cream, 29
Croissants, *30–1*, 52–5
Crumpets, *30–1*, 61
Crust, 41, 44, 49
Currants, 29, 70, 72, 76–7, 84

Dates, 29, 76

Easter breads, 26–7, *30–1*, 84–5
Eastern Europe, 80
Eggs, 25
Elasticity of dough, 12
Endosperm, 13
England, 26–7, 60
Equipment, baking, 16–17, 56, 70
Experimental grain farm, *18*

Fat, 6, 20, 25
Fault-finding, 88–91
Ferment and Dough method, 32–3, 42–3
Fermentation process, 24–5, 28, 43
Festive loaves, 26–7
see also special loaves
Fibre, 20
Final proof, 34, 36
Flour, *13–15*, 18–21
Flying Sponge method, 44
Four piece loaf, *30–1*, 62–3
France, 11
French bread, *30–1*, 78–9
Freezing, 83
Fruit brioches, 56
Fruit breads, *30–1*, 69–77
Fruit, dried, 29, 70, 72, 75–7, 84
Fruit malt bread, *30–1*, 75

Germ wheat, 13, 30
Germ meal, 20
Germany, 26–7
Gluten, 9, 12, 24, 38
Good Friday bun
see Hot cross buns
Grains for bread, 12–13, 19
Granaries, *6–7*
Granary flour, 21
Greece, 26

Ham croissants, 55
Holland, 26
Honey, 8
Hot cross buns, 26–7, *30–1*, 84–5

India, *15*
Intermediate rising, 34, 36
International recipes, 78–83
Iron, 20
Italy, 26

Jewish breads, 80, 86–7

Kneading, 34, 38

Lattice tea bread, *30–1*, 72
Lox and bagel, 87

Maize, 12
Malt, 25, 29
Malt bread, *30–1*, 75
Marzipan, 74
Measurement, correct, 41
Methods of breadmaking, 32–44
Middle East, 11
Milk, 8, 25, 44
Millet, 12
Milling, *14–15*, 21
Mixing, 41
Moulding dough, 34, 39
Muffins, *30–1*, 60, 86

94

New Year breads, 26
Nicotinic acid, 20
Nutmeg, 29, 77, 84
Nutrients in bread, 6, 20
Nuts, 71, 74, 76

Onion bagel, 87
Oven bottom cakes, *30–1*, 49

Peel, mixed, 77, 84
Pericarp, 13
Pikelets, 61
Pizza base (wholewheat), 83
Plaited loaves, *30–1*, 62–8, 71
Poland, 26
Protein, 6, 20
Prunes, 29, 76
Punching down, 34

Raisins, 29, 70, 72, 75–7, 84
Recipes:
 basic, 32–3, 40–4;
 fruit breads, 69–77;
 international, 78–83;
 special, 52–61;
 traditional, 46–51;
 twists and plaits, 62–8
Riboflavin, 20
Rising, 35–7
Rolls, 65
Round loaves, *30–1*, 39, 48
Russia, 26
Rye, 12, 22, 80–1
Rye bread, *30–1*, 80

Saffron, 29
Salt, 20, 24–5, 41
Skinning of dough, 36, 77
Special loaves, *26–7*, 52–61
Spices, 29, 77, 84
Stale bread, freshening, 79
Starch, 13
Sticky buns, *30–1*, 74
Stollen, *30–1*, 74–5
Stone ground flour, 21–3

Straight Dough method, 32–3, 40–1
Strong flour, 18, 22
Sugar, 25
Sweet and sour bread, *30–1*, 81

Tea bread, Lattice, *30–1*, 72
Techniques of breadmaking, 32–44
Temperature, 36–7, 43
Testing: baked bread, 35; dough, 37
Thiamin, 20
Tin bread, 37, 39
Tins, 56, 70
Tips, 41, 43
Tools *see* equipment
Tortillas, 12
Traditional recipes, 46–51
Twisted loaves, *30–1*, 62–68

Vitamin C, 24

Walnut fruit loaf, *30–1*, 76
Welsh fruit loaf, 77
Wheat, 12–13
Wheat germ, 13, 20
White bread, 20
Wholewheat, 20–3
Wholewheat bread, 9, 21–3, *30–1*, 51
Wholewheat pizza base, 83

Yeast, 8–9, 25, 28–9
Yorkshire tea cakes, *30–1*, 71

INDEX OF RECIPES

Apple Köcken, 73
Bagels, 86–7
Bara-brith, 77
Beer bread, 82
Bloomer, 47
Brioche, 56–9
Brown bread, 50
Chelsea tea ring, 74
Cinnamon slice, 73
Coburg, 48
Coil, 68
Cottage, loaf, 47
Croissants, 52–8
Crumpets, 61
Four piece loaf, 62–3
French bread, 78–9
Fruit loaves,
 basic recipe, 71
Fruit malt loaf, 75
Fruit plaits, 71
Hot cross buns, 84–5
Lattice tea bread, 22
Muffins, 60
Oven bottom cakes, 49
Pizza base, 83
Plaits,
 basic recipe, 62
 variations, 63–6
Round, 48
Rye, bread, 80
Sticky buns, 72
Stollen, 74
Sweet and sour bread, 81
Traditional loaves,
 basic recipe, 46
Twists, 67
Wholewheat bread, 51
Walnut fruit loaf, 76
Yorkshire tea cakes, 71

Acknowledgments

The 'How To' Book of
Bread and Breadmaking was
created by Simon Jennings
and Company Limited.
We are grateful to the
following individuals and
organizations for their
assistance in the making
of this book:

Lindsay Blow: *all line illustrations*
John Couzins: *cover and title page photographs, and pages 17, 19, 23, 29, 31, 59, 65*
The Dover Archive: *engravings and embellishments*
Mary Evans Picture Library: *engravings on pages 9 and 11*
The Flour Advisory Bureau: *statistical information*
Ann Hall: *compilation of index*
Christopher Perry: *additional artwork*
Dee Robinson: *picture research*
The Scolar Press: *engravings from 'Art For Commerce'*

Photographs:
Barnaby Picture Library: page 11 *bl*
J. Allen Cash: pages 6 *t*; 7 *r*; 10 *b*; 14 *b*; 15 *all*; 27 *tr*
Mary Evans: page 6 *b*
Robert Harding Associates: pages 6 *c*; 10 *c*; 11 *bl*; 14 *t*
Rank Hovis MacDougall: pages 10 *t*; 11 *br*; 18 *t* and *c*
Spectrum Picture Library: pages 26 *t* and *b*; 27 *tl* and *b*

abbreviations: *t* top; *b* bottom; *c* center; *tl* top left; *tr* top right; *bl* bottom left; *br* bottom right; *r* right

Typesetting by Servis Filmsetting Ltd., Manchester
Headline setting by Facet Photosetting, London

Special thanks to Norman Ruffell and
the staff of Swaingrove Ltd., Bury St. Edmunds,
Suffolk, for the lithographic reproduction.

'HOW TO'